D0098326

A MIRROR FOR MAGISTRATES *AND THE* DE CASIBUS *TRADITION*

THE MENTAL AND CULTURAL WORLD OF TUDOR AND STUART ENGLAND

Editors

Paul Christianson
Camille Slights
D.R. Woolf

PAUL BUDRA

A Mirror for Magistrates and the *de casibus* Tradition

UNIVERSITY OF TORONTO PRESS
Toronto Buffalo London

© University of Toronto Press Incorporated 2000
Toronto Buffalo London
Printed in Canada

ISBN 0-8020-4717-3

∞

Printed on acid-free paper

Canadian Cataloguing in Publication Data

Budra, Paul Vincent, 1957–
A mirror for magistrates and the de casibus tradition

(The mental and cultural world of Tudor and Stuart England)
Includes bibliographical references and index.
ISBN 0-8020-4717-3

1. Mirror for magistrates. 2. Great Britain – Historiography.
3. Great Britain – History – Sources. I. Title. II. Series.

PR2199.M53B82 2000   821'.3   C99-932870-0

University of Toronto Press acknowledges the financial assistance to its
publishing program of the Canada Council for the Arts and the Ontario
Arts Council.

This book has been published with the help of a grant from the Humanities
and Social Sciences Federation of Canada, using funds provided by the Social
Sciences and Humanities Research Council of Canada.

University of Toronto Press acknowledges the financial support for its
publishing activities of the Government of Canada through the Book
Publishing Industry Development Program (BPIDP).

Canadä

For Karen, my mirror

Contents

Acknowledgments

Parts of this book have appeared in journal form. I am grateful to the editors of *Philological Quarterly* and *Renaissance & Reformation* for permission to use this material. Parts of the introduction and chapter 1 appeared as 'The *Mirror for Magistrates* and the Shape of *de casibus* Tragedy' in *English Studies* 69/4 (1988): 303–12, used with permission of Swets & Zeitlinger. Parts of chapter 2 appeared as 'The *Mirror for Magistrates* and the Politics of Readership,' in *Studies in English Literature, 1500–1900* 32 (1992): 1–13, copyright *SEL*, reprinted by permission of Johns Hopkins University Press.

Simon Fraser University has supported the production of this book with a President's Research Grant that allowed me to hire very fine research assistants. My thanks to them. I would like to thank the members of the Pacific Northwest Renaissance Society, who heard the first rumblings of what would become this book and who offered sage advice and support. And many thanks to Professor Daniel Woolf, who has been especially supportive of this project.

PAUL BUDRA

Introduction

Why write a book on *A Mirror for Magistrates*? The scholarly interest in the book has tended to be archeological, and the limited critical reaction has been almost uniformly apologetic. The text has been thoroughly excavated as the source for later dramatic tragedies, but those critics who have focused on the work for itself have isolated a few points of poetic interest, notably the 'Induction' and 'The Tragedy of Buckingham,' both by Thomas Sackville, and dismissed the rest. This dismissal has taken two forms: either the individual tragedies are shown to be predictable stories of the schematic retribution inflicted upon the morally or politically corrupt,[1] and are therefore consistent and tedious, or they are shown to be a haphazard assortment of tales mixing divine providence with irrational fortune, and are therefore inconsistent and tedious.[2]

This dismissal is unfortunate but understandable. Critics fascinated with Elizabethan and Jacobean tragedy have looked back to the *Mirror* as a proto-tragedy, a primitive stage in the evolution towards, above all, Shakespearean tragedy. This trend was in part mitigated by the twentieth-century editor of the *Mirror*, Lily B. Campbell, who argued that

> the *Mirror for Magistrates* was an important pioneer work in literature, because it transferred to the poet the accepted task of the historian – a task which, if the defenders of poetry are to be believed, he could perform more delightfully, more directly, and hence more effectively, than could the historian ... The importance of this transfer of the function of political teaching from the historian to the poet ... can, however, be fully realized only when consideration is given to the long line of historical plays and poems popular during the reign of Elizabeth.[3]

So, even for Campbell, the *Mirror* was, at best, a pioneering work that pointed to later drama. But to treat the *Mirror* as a precursor of the drama is a mistake for two reasons. First, the book was not antecedent to the drama; it was still being published in new editions as Shakespeare was writing. Second, this enforced hindsight, with its implications of evolutionary progress, has imposed formal expectations on the *de casibus* literary tradition that have nothing to do with that tradition's own history. To treat the *Mirror* simply as a piece of primitive tragic literature is to misunderstand the significant literary tradition that it epitomized, not pioneered. Campbell was right to emphasize the importance of the work as history writing, and scholars of Elizabethan historiography inevitably make passing reference to the *Mirror*, but literary critics continue to categorize the work by inappropriate literary taxonomies that marginalize and diminish the work's significance.[4] This book is a first step towards correcting that mistake.

Further, the banishment of the *Mirror* to the footnotes of teaching editions of English Renaissance plays has deprived scholars of a rich addition to the current critical debates on the early modern period. While recent literary criticism of the English Renaissance has been dominated by questions of nation building, of the relation of power to cultural production, and of the politics of subjectivity, these discussions have tended to circle around Sidney, Spenser, and the dramatists of the public theatres. This is the case, not because current scholars are re-advocating the canon – far from it – but because the literature of these Renaissance writers has a cultural resonance that arises, in part, from those writers' variation and manipulation of literary forms with familiar genealogies – genealogies that have continued, in some cases, into the twentieth century. By delineating the form of *de casibus* literature, I hope to establish its genealogy and the concomitant formal expectations by which the *Mirror* should be evaluated. Only with such a history at hand can we understand the successes and failures of manifestations of *de casibus* literature, such as the *Mirror*, and begin to assess their value to the discussions that are now preoccupying Renaissance scholars. I hope to suggest, in the last chapters of this book, that the *Mirror* can add much to such discussions.

The book begins with an overview of the *Mirror*'s complicated publication history and its relation to its precursors. This is a hurdle that must be crossed, for at least some of the scholarly reluctance to treat the *Mirror* in depth seems tied to its complex life at the press. It should also suggest the degree to which the *Mirror* was of a kind with some of the better-known, more thoroughly studied, texts of the Tudor age. Like Foxe's *Book of Martyrs* and Holinshed's *Chronicles*, the *Mirror* was a patriotic and political work that passed through the hands of multiple editors and contributors over a long printing history. This sort of complex literary endeavour, so indicative of mid-sixteenth-century print culture and suggestive of early modern understanding of text, narrative, and history, needs to be further studied by scholars of early modern publishing, literature, and history writing.

Chapter 2 puts forward the main argument of the book: that the *Mirror* is part of the tradition of *de casibus* literature. By 'de casibus literature,' I mean those works written in direct imitation of the form of Boccaccio's *De casibus virorum illustrium*. That tradition, I will argue, was not based on ideas or forms of tragedy. Rather, *de casibus* literature was a form of history writing that used concatenated biographies to demonstrate a teleology (in the theological sense of that word) at work in the course of human events. It could be, and, as we shall see, often was, overtly political in intent, for the form combined the *Fürstenspiegel* ('Mirror for Princes,' or counsel book) format with the exemplary mode to offer a polemical reading of history. This means that, to understand the evolution of the *Mirror* over its publishing history, we have to place it in the context of late Tudor and early Stuart historiographic innovation. The various authors of the *Mirror* assumed that *de casibus* literature was a form of history writing and worked, or at least purported to work, within the intellectual parameters of contemporaneous historiography. As we shall see, the authors of the early editions of the *Mirror* were aware of the economies of prestige and authority that delimited both the authorial voice (especially when engaged with history) and class or political prerogative, and used this knowledge as part of their polemic.

In chapter 3 I look at how *de casibus* became associated with both tragedy and the discussion of fortune. This association was confused by the various authors' erratic understanding of the literary terms they employed and the slipperiness of the concept of fortune itself. Chaucer is important to the history of this association. Indeed, he is more important than most Chaucer critics have noticed, for they, like so many critics of Tudor drama, have consistently failed to evaluate *de casibus* literature, including Chaucer's *Monk's Tale*, by the formal criterion that its practitioners assumed. The alignment of *de casibus* with tragedy is also important as an indication of the degree to which tragedy and history ran together in the Renaissance mind, ran together to such a point that critics such as Irving Ribner have declared that it is impossible to distinguish, for example, the history play from tragedy as dramatic genre.[5] Renaissance thinkers, influenced by a pervasive sense of universal decay resulting from the Fall, found it difficult to avoid images of decline and catastrophe in their depiction of individual historical lives or empires. The significance of this popular assumption – that history was tragic, and tragedy recounted history – has been insufficiently studied by critics of the English Renaissance. The *Mirror* is a propitious text with which to begin such a study.

Chapters 4 and 5 offer critical applications of my understanding of *de casibus* literature. The first application is to the question of the representation of gender in the *Mirror*. I hope to demonstrate that it was the formal expectations of *de casibus*, more than the content of individual tales, that had ideological implications for the representation of women. In chapter 5, I come back to the question of the *Mirror* and drama, but rather than revisit the archeological work done on the text, I tackle two facets of this relationship that have not been discussed. First, I look at the influence of drama on the *Mirror*. Second, I offer a preliminary example of what can be done with drama and the *Mirror* once the historical import of the *de casibus* form is acknowledged. I offer an overview of Shakespeare's most famous history plays that relies on this interpretation of *de casibus* literature, and then a more sustained reading of Shakespeare's *Richard II*. With it I hope to demonstrate what approaches to some of the best-known literature of the English Renaissance may be possible when those works are reflected in a new *Mirror*.

A MIRROR FOR MAGISTRATES AND
THE *DE CASIBUS* TRADITION

Chapter One

Printing the *Mirror*

In 1553, John Wayland returned to the printing business by buying the Sign of the Sun, a London printing house recently owned by Edward Whitchurch, a Protestant who had left the business during Mary I's Catholic reign. Wayland, a staunch Catholic from Middlesex, had been out of the printing business for almost fifteen years; he had spent those years working as a scrivener, bookseller, and professional litigant embroiled in a series of complicated suits involving land title, loan defaults, and book deals. He may have returned to printing because he had secured a patent, presumably through the influence of a friend at court, to be the sole printer of all primers and prayer manuals in England for seven years. But primers and prayerbooks were not all he was to print, and a good thing too: his monopoly was infringed upon by at least six other printers during the reign of Mary.[1]

The first major secular printing project Wayland undertook was an edition of John Lydgate's *Fall of Princes*, a work that had most recently been printed in 1527 by Richard Pynson.[2] Wayland explained his rationale for the project this way: 'because that sundry gentlemen very wel lerned, commended much the workes of Lydgate, chefely the fal of Prynces, which he drew out of Bochas [Boccaccio], whereof none were to be got, after that I knew the Counsayles pleasure & aduice therein, I determined to print it.'[3] In fact, the decision to reprint Lydgate's work may have had more to do with the stock of Wayland's printing house than with the opinions of learned gentlemen. The Sign of the Sun, a Fleet Street house that had once belonged to Wynkyn de Worde, had recently been the centre of some financial wrangling. When Whitchurch went out of business in 1553, the house was first bought by the printers William and Humphrey Powell. They ran into financial and legal problems during their brief ownership and seem to have sold off stock, including some of the material for an edition of *Fall of Princes* that Whitchurch himself had hoped to bring out that very year. Some of this stock ended up in the hands of Richard Tottel, a publisher of law books who would go on to become famous for publishing *Songs and Sonnets* (1557), a collection of short verse that eventually became known as *Tottel's Miscellany*. The rest went to Wayland when he took over the printing house. Both Wayland and Tottel brought out editions of *Fall of Princes* in 1554.

To understand why Whitchurch, Tottel, and Wayland would want to print *Fall of Princes*, we first need to understand its history and reputation. This endeavour takes us back to fourteenth-century Italy.

In the aftermath of the Black Plague of 1348, Giovanni Boccaccio was turning his back on the wry literature of love that had made him famous and that has become his most popular work. This movement away from vernacular, secular literature was given extra urgency by the 1362 visit of Gioacchino Ciani, a Carthusian monk, who claimed to come from Pietro Petroni, a renowned holy man who had recently died. Ciani said that Petroni had seen Boccaccio's imminent death in a vision and had concluded that, unless the poet repent his sins and turn to more Christian labours, his damnation was assured. Deeply disturbed by this news, Boccaccio considered renouncing the world entirely in favour of ascetic retreat. He was prevented by the common sense of his friend Francesco Petrarch, who argued that learning is never in vain and could serve holy ends: 'All history is full of examples of good men who have loved learning, and though many unlettered men have attained to holiness, no man was ever debarred from holiness by letters.'[4] Accordingly, Boccaccio gave up writing in Italian for the eternal and universal language of Latin; he gave up raillery for scholarship; he gave up licentiousness for piety.

It is for the serious Latin works of his last years that Boccaccio was best known and admired during the Renaissance. Many of these works are compilations: *De genealogie deorum gentilium* is a vast collection of classical myths combined with a defence of poetry – one of the earliest compendiums of classical mythology; *De montibus* is a collection of Boccaccio's geographical knowledge. But the first of the serious Latin books Boccaccio wrote was historical, and it was to be his most popular: *De casibus virorum illustrium*. In this work, Boccaccio narrated a dream vision, but it was a dream vision very unlike the one he used in his earlier profane work *Amorosa Visione*. This was a vision of the famous men and women of history, from Adam and Eve to his contemporary Jean le Bon, who had fallen on Fortune's wheel. They appeared to him, lamenting their fates and reciting their sad stories; he dutifully copied down, in nine books, those tales that were the most instructive of fortune's instability.

De casibus was written between 1356 and 1360 and revised in 1373. It was dedicated in 1363 or 1364 to a Florentine named Mainardo dei Cavalcanti because, Boccaccio explained, there was no living ruler, secular or religious, worthy of the tribute. Boccaccio's sources for the work were classical historians such as Livy, Valerius Maximus, Curtius Rufus, Suetonius, Tacitus, Solinus, Godfrey of Viterbo, and Eusebius. He also used classical poets (most notably Ovid), the Bible, Latin Christian authors such as Saint Isiodore, and some more recent European historians, especially Fra Paolino da Venezia. Boccaccio may have derived the form of the book from the fourth-century *De mortibus persecutorum* of Lactantius. That work chronicled the unfortunate fates of those Roman emperors who persecuted Christians. Also important to the form was the tradition of classical biography as epitomized in Plutarch's *Parallel Lives*. Plutarch recited, in short order but with strong moralizing tone, the lives of forty-six Greek and Roman personages, drawing parallels and contrasts between their characters. Influential to Boccaccio's philosophical thought were Seneca's *De consolatione*, Boethius's *De consolatione philosophiae*, and Macrobius's *Somnium scipionis*.[5] Finally, he may have drawn inspiration from his friend Petrarch's *De viris illustribus*, written just a few years before he began the *De casibus*. Given the scope and solemnity of the *De casibus*, it is not surprising then that 'for the men of the fifteenth century Boccaccio was the great moralist, comparable to Boethius and Seneca,' and that the work as a whole was so influential that, in Spain, for example, it was quoted beside Genesis and the works of Saint Augustine.[6] This popularity meant that the book was translated, and, as it was translated, it was transformed.

The first significant translation was undertaken by Laurent de Premierfait (1380?–1418), an ecclesiastic clerk from the province of Champagne who had gained a reputation as a poet and Latin scholar. He moved in humanist circles and eventually found work translating for noble patrons. He translated *De casibus* in 1400, and then again in 1409 as *De Cas de Nobles Hommes et Femmes*. *De Cas* is almost three times longer than *De casibus*. Premierfait expanded names, gave dates, introduced explanatory phrases, inserted connectives, and expanded chapter introductions. He also inserted moral interpolations.[7] This process of expansion was planned and methodical: Premierfait explained in the prologue of the second edition that he could better please his readers by amplifying than by giving a literal translation of the Latin. The result was a translation so free that it should probably be considered a new work,[8] but it was through this very loose French translation that *De casibus* became known in England.

It was probably in 1431, while he was acting as the lieutenant and warden of England for Henry VI, who was in France, that Humphrey, Duke of Gloucester, asked John Lydgate to translate *De casibus* into English. Lydgate was a peasant from Suffolk who had been recruited to the Abbey of St Edmunds in the mid-1380s. He was ordained in 1397 and shortly thereafter began a literary career that would take him from his home base of the monastery of Bury into court circles and onto the Continent. His patrons would include Henry V, Thomas Montacute, William de la Poole, Lady Talbot, and Lady March. He used Premierfait's second French version of *De casibus* as the basis for a Boccaccio 'translation' titled *Fall of Princes*. Between 1432 and 1438 Lydgate rendered the French prose work into English poetry, 36,365 lines of decasyllabic verse in rhyme royal. Like Premierfait, he felt no compunction about altering his source material, although he promised to be true to his original: 'Yit fro the trouthe shal I nat remue, / But on the substane bi good leiser abide, / Afftier myn auctour lik as I may atteyne' (1: 231–3).[9] He deleted various sections of his source, most notably the stories of Priam and Troy (Lydgate had already written on this subject in his *Troy Book* for his then patron, Henry V), and Agamemnon and Menelaus. He made various patriotic changes to ensure that the English rulers were represented in a better light than they had been by both Premierfait and Boccaccio.[10] He was quick to praise the descendants of his patron, such as Edward III. He showed an appropriately monkish reticence about sexuality and was embarrassed by the passages by Boccaccio and Premierfait that railed against women.[11]

Humphrey, who was one of the most important patrons of his age, seems to have overseen the translation with some care. It was he who suggested that Lydgate write explanatory 'envoys' at the beginning of sections of the text. These envoys would prove to be among the most popular things in the book, so popular that in 1519 Wynkyn de Worde published *The Prouerbes of Lydgate*, a collection of the poet's pithier musings, largely derived from *Fall of Princes* envoys. Humphrey also lent Lydgate source books, such as John of Salisbury's *Policraticus*,

from his own library. In return, Lydgate praised him in the prologue
and epilogue as 'bothe manli and eek wis, / Chose off God to been his
owyn knyht' (1: 407–8) and mentioned him in passing in the envoys as
an exemplum of generosity and sage leadership:

> And a-mong bookis, pleyni this the cas,
> This said[e] prynce considred off resoun,
> The noble book of this Iohn Bochas
> Was, accordyng in his opynyoun,
> Off gret noblesse and reputacioun,
> And onto pryncis gretli necessarie
> To yiue exaumple how this world doth varie.   (1: 421–7)[12]

Because Boccaccio's Latin original was never circulated widely in
England, *Fall of Princes* was *De casibus* for the majority of English readers. It was published under Boccaccio's name. It was well known, first
in manuscript and, starting in 1494, in print, when Richard Pynson, a
London printer from Middlesex who began in the trade by reprinting
Caxton's editions of Chaucer's *Canterbury Tales*, printed Lydgate's
work in a handsome folio edition adorned with woodcuts at the
request of John Russhe, a London merchant with whom he had some
unfortunate business dealings. Pynson printed it again in 1527, a year
before he left the printing business.[13]

The book was popular enough to inspire imitations. Around 1552–4
George Cavendish (1499?–1562?), a former gentleman usher to Cardinal Wolsey who had retired to Suffolk, wrote *Metrical Visions*, a collection of verse tragedies that drew heavily on *Fall of Princes* and that
seems to have been conceived as an adornment for his prose biography
of the great cardinal.[14] A much smaller work than Lydgate's, *Metrical
Visions* copied *Fall of Princes*, and therefore Boccaccio, by having ghosts
complain to the narrator about their terrible fates. Cavendish introduced two innovations. First, he focused on near contemporaries,
many of whom he knew personally. The first ghost to appear is Lord
Wolsey himself, who, after relating his rise from obscurity to power,
rues the contrast between his former worldly glories and his present
state: 'Ffarewell Hampton Court / whos ffounder I was / Ffarewell
Westmynster Place / nowe a palace Royall' (232–3).[15] Second, Cavendish allowed the ghosts to talk in the first person rather that retelling
their complaints after the fact, as had, for the most part, Boccaccio and
Lydgate.

So, when Whitchurch, Tottel, and Wayland decided to reissue *Fall of Princes*, they were hoping for a success based on the reputation of *De casibus* as one of the great books of the Continental Renaissance. Tottel's edition came out 10 September 1554, and while Wayland's edition cannot be so firmly dated, it came out around the same time.[16] Whatever the dating, Wayland's edition, based on Pynson's second edition of 1527, was the superior book.

The superiority of the Wayland edition of *Fall of Princes* may, in part, have been the result of another piece of stock that Wayland inherited from Whitchurch: a corrector by the name of William Baldwin (d. 1563?). Baldwin was an Oxford graduate with influential friends who was already gaining a reputation as a poet while in university. He would be listed in the 1556 charter incorporating the Stationers' Company.[17] He was a soldier who served in Scotland and Ireland. And he was a scholar. His 1547 book *Moral Philosophy* was so popular it underwent ten editions under Baldwin's guidance in Whitchurch's printing house, and numerous others under a pirate named Thomas Paulfreyman. Baldwin had translated *Ballads of Solomon* (1549); his *Beware the Cat* (1553, but not published until 1560) would draw controversy as a religious satire. Later his *Funeralles of King Edward the Sixth* (1560) would be suppressed – and therefore well known – for seven years. From 1552 to 1556 he was associated, through his friend George Ferrers, Master of the King's Pastimes, with the Court Revels. He was involved in the Court Christmas celebrations of 1552 and would write plays for Court, including a highly elaborate spectacle for Christmas 1556. He would become respected enough as an historian to be asked to help John Stow in his *Summarie* (1565).[18] Jasper Heywood would later write,

> In Lyncolnes Inne and Temples twayne,
>   Grayes Inne and other mo ...
> There heare thou shalt a great reporte,
>   of Baldwyns worthie name,
> Whose Myrrour dothe of Magistrates,
>   proclayme eternall fame.[19]

Even in 1554 Baldwin was on his way to becoming a literary personality, and it was probably this potential, combined with his influential connections, that overcame the religious differences between him and his employer. Wayland would have been foolish to oust Baldwin, even if the man was a rabid Protestant.[20]

Baldwin was the perfect man to execute an idea Wayland had to
make his edition of *Fall of Princes* especially appealing, an idea that he
may have conjured to best Tottel. He decided that he would extend the
De casibus formula into recent English history. That is, he would have
the chronological frame of the work expanded, adding tragedies based
on the lives of English historical figures. He wanted 'to haue the storye
contynewed from where as Bochas lefte, vnto this presente time,
chiefly of suche as Fortune had dalyed with here in this ylande' (1: 68).
This was a savvy publishing move. History books were strong sellers.
But Baldwin was no monk of Bury; he was not about to take the years
necessary to write a poetic chronicle of English history by himself. So,
as he explains,

> because it was a matter passyng my wyt and skyll, and more thankles
> than gaineful to meddle in, I refused vtterly to vndertake it, excepte I
> might haue the helpe of suche, as in wyt were apte, in learning allowed,
> and in iudgemente and estymacion able to wield and furnysh so weighty
> an enterpryse, thinkyng euen so to shift my handes. But he earnest and
> diligent in his affayres, procured Athlas to set vnder his shoulder: for
> shortly after, dyuers learned men whose many giftes nede fewe praises,
> consented to take vpon theym part of the trauayle. And whan certayne of
> theym to the numbre of seuen, were throughe a generall assent at an
> apoynted time and place gathered together to deuyse therupon, I resorted
> vnto them, bering with me the booke of Bochas, translated by Dan Lid-
> gate, for the better obseruacion of his order. (1: 68–9)

The seven men gathered, and their first piece of business was to elect
someone to chair the proceedings. They agreed that Baldwin should
'vsurpe Bochas rowme' (1: 69). He was made not only the master of
ceremonies for the construction of the text at hand, but also the book's
dominant literary persona. The lamenting figures of the tragedies were
to report to him. And, as Cavendish had done, Baldwin and his successors had their ghosts speak in the first person, reciting the stories of
their lives from the grave directly to Baldwin rather than having the
vision explained after the fact as, for the most part, Boccaccio and his
translators had done. Whether or not Baldwin et al. borrowed the idea
from Cavendish or arrived at it separately is unknown. *Metrical Visions*
was not published in Cavendish's lifetime; indeed, it was not published in full until the nineteenth century. If the first writers of the
Mirror knew the work, it could only have been the manuscript version,

but the chances that the urban authors of the *Mirror* were familiar with the reclusive Cavendish seem slight. Whatever the case, this device, besides offering the possibility of psychological portrayal (all too infrequently made use of), greatly increased the didactic potential of the individual stories. The ghosts, in reflecting upon their lives, could draw morals directly from their own past actions. There is hardly a story that does not end with some variation of the sentiment in this stanza spoken by the ghost of Lord Mowbray:

> Note here the ende of pride, se Flateries fine,
> Marke the reward of enuy and false complaint,
> And warne all princes from them to declyne
> Lest likely fault do find the like attaynt.
> Let this my life be to them a restraynt,
> By others harmes who lysteth take no hede
> Shall by his owne learne other better rede.   (1: 109)

When the moral was insufficiently explicit, the authors reiterated the point in the prose links between the poems, often citing other historical parallels for emphasis. These links are not the exact equivalent of Lydgate's envoys. Those were poetic passages that surveyed or summarized the material at hand. The prose links that Baldwin used are much more eclectic: they discuss source materials, historical controversies, questions of metrics, or the upcoming tragedy.

The collection contained a total of nineteen tragedies that covered roughly the period of the War of the Roses, beginning with Robert Tresilian and ending with Edward IV. This time frame was chosen, we are told in the first prose link, because it begins approximately where Boccaccio concludes (1: 69). When the new tragedies were added to the new Lydgate edition, then, Wayland would have a mammoth and encyclopedic book stretching from Adam and Eve to Edward IV.

But that is not what happened. The new tragedies, called as a collection *A Mirror for Magistrates*, were not printed with the new Lydgate edition. Indeed, the book seems to have been stopped in mid-printing by government censors. The reasons for the restriction, discussed in the next chapter, were bound up in Baldwin's Protestant revision of history. But we can imagine how upset Wayland must have been. Here he was, not only a Catholic, but a Catholic with the patent to be the sole printer of all primers and prayer manuals in England, having his work not only hindered, but hindered for Protestant sedition. He must have distanced himself from the publication immediately, because he was successful in renewing his patent in 1556. He stayed in the printing business for a few more years, bringing out an edition of *The Pastime of Pleasure* (1554) (again in contest with Richard Tottel, who brought out the same book a year later) and *The Dial of Princes* (1557), and even reissuing Baldwin's hit, *Moral Philosophy*. But eventually his litigious nature got the best of him, and by 1558 he was spending time in jail and sinking into debts incurred through bad business deals and doomed lawsuits. He probably died, certainly poor, in 1572.

The *Mirror* would not be published for five years and, even then, parts of it would be repressed. It would take a change of monarch and printer to get the *Mirror* out.

The printer who finally put the *Mirror* onto the bookstalls was Thomas Marshe. Marshe had had an eclectic early career. He printed everything, from psalters to cookbooks. Later he would have success in history and tragedy. He would print, in 1559, for William Seres, a book titled *An Epitome of Chronicles*, a 750-page quarto historical overview based on the 1549 work by Thomas Lanquet and Thomas Cooper.[21] But he is probably best known to students of Renaissance literature as the printer of *Seneca His Tenne Tragedies* (1581). That book was edited by Thomas Newton, who brought together earlier translations of individual plays by John Studley, Alexander Nevile, T. Nuce, and Jasper Heywood, and added his own translation of *Thebias*. It was to have a profound influence on the practice of English drama. Marshe's predilection for history and tragedy may have arisen out of the success of the *Mirror*, a book that was at once a historical overview and a collection of tragedies.

Marshe brought out the *Mirror* in 1559, but not all of it. Some of the tragedies were still too politically sensitive to see print. 'Edmund, Duke of Somerset' was not printed until the 1563 edition. The tale of Elianor Cobham was also suppressed. It seems to have been written as an analogy of the experiences of Elizabeth and Dr John Dee in 1555 and 1556. The author of this particular tale, Baldwin's friend George Ferrers, actually served as a Privy Council informant against the young Elizabeth.[22] It was not published, nor was the tale of Humphrey Plantagenet, the Duke of Gloucester, until 1578.

The book, however truncated, was a popular success, and that meant that a series of editions was printed over the next few years, many of them adding tragedies that had been suppressed in the original edition. Subsequent Baldwin editions took the stories up to the time of Wolsey. But as these editions were coming out, Marshe started another project. While Wayland had had the idea of extending the chronology of Lydgate, Marshe seems to have had the idea of extending the scope of the *Mirror* to cover all of English history. And so, in 1575, Marshe printed *The First Part of the Mirror for Magistrates*, a collection of tragic tales written by John Higgins that covered the historical period from Brute, the legendary founder of Britain, descendant of the Trojan exile Aeneas, until Caesar. Higgins was a young Oxford graduate who combined a gift for languages with an antiquarian bent. In the introduction to his edition, he claims to have been motivated by Baldwin's musing in the original *Mirror* that 'it were ... a goodly and notable matter to search and discourse our whole story from the beginninge of the inhabiting of this Isle' (2: 37). This prequel to the *Mirror* was printed twice and then fused together with the original *Mirror* for an edition in 1587.

The success of the *Mirror* project inspired other printers. In 1578 a printer named Richard Webster brought out a work titled *The Second Part of the Mirror for Magistrates*. The author of this text, Thomas Blennerhasset, covered the time from the Roman Conquest until William the Conqueror. Blennerhasset, a soldier from a good family (his brother was knighted in 1603), had studied at Cambridge. He was stationed on the Isle of Guernsey, where he served under Sir Thomas Leighton and, eventually, ended up a landowner of some consequence in Ireland. Webster himself seems fated not to have been a printer; after working for Thomas Dawson, a printer who specialized in catechisms, he brought out the Blennerhasset book under his name and left the trade.

Finally, in 1610, Felix Kyngston brought out *A Winter Nights Vision* by Richard Niccols. Kyngston was a prolific and long-lived printer whose specialty was religious materials. Niccols was an Oxford graduate and Spenser enthusiast who began his career as an undergraduate writing on the death of Elizabeth. The *Mirror* project was by far the largest thing he ever attempted in verse.[23] He would later write at least one play, and other antiquarian and topical poems. Niccols filled in gaps in the chronology left after Baldwin's, Higgins's, and Blennerhasset's works were all compiled: he wrote a King Arthur narrative; rewrote the Richard III tragedy; and included 'England's Eliza,' a long poem in praise of Queen Elizabeth.

So, between 1559 and 1610, the *Mirror* went through four editors. It expanded in size to accommodate virtually all of British history. Like

Foxe's *Book of Martyrs* and Holinshed's *Chronicles*, it was the product of a complex intersection of sources, writers, and printers. As a combination of poetry, history, and political censure, it was highly esteemed by contemporaries. Meres ranked it, in *Palladis Tamia* (1598), along with the works of Shakespeare, Marlowe, Kyd, Chapman, Dekker, and Jonson; Sidney praised its 'bewtiful partes';[24] and Ben Jonson mentioned it in the prologue to *Bartholomew Fair* some four years after the final *Mirror* edition was printed. Baldwin, as we have seen, was lauded for the work, and Elizabethan dramatists regularly used the *Mirror* as an archive of material. And it was widely imitated: various other 'Mirrors' were printed using some variation of the *Mirror* formula; the popular 'lament' tradition evolved in response to the example of the *Mirror*'s autobiographical complaints.[25] But above all, the *Mirror* was influential because of the vision of history it offered. To understand the text, then, we must first understand its significance as a piece of history writing.

Chapter Two

History

Lily B. Campbell, in her article 'Tudor Conceptions of History and Tragedy in *A Mirror for Magistrates*,' reminds us that the Renaissance employed history, and historically oriented texts such as the *Mirror*, as a source of 'immediately useful' information. She intimates that the reason for the inordinate faith placed in the value of history was theoretical: history was viewed as repetitive, or cyclical, and therefore major patterns of events could be counted on to recur.[1] Whether this assumption was the product of an articulated philosophy of history or the fruit of an unexpressed worldly wisdom, Campbell does not make clear. Certainly such writers as Samuel Daniel, who was fascinated with images of cyclical alteration of empires and seasons, seem to argue for such a model of history.[2] Certain classical scholars and those conversant with the avant-garde of Italian historiography might also have been tempted into adopting the Graeco-Roman conception of history as an endless series of cyclical revolutions. But, for most people, the notion of cyclical time would have occurred only in the contemplation of natural, liturgical, and metaphorical patterns of recurrence, none of which would have superseded the orthodox Christian perception of history as a finite progression of events from the Creation to the Apocalypse.[3] Time, for the Christian, is linear and progressive; a gradual revelation of God's purpose in specific events; a diptych structure articulated at the point of the Incarnation.[4] The contrast between the two theories was most pointedly expressed by Augustine, who ridiculed supporters of the cyclical theory in Book XII of *The City of God*.[5] The insistence upon a linear model of history was adopted by Luther and lost none of its prevalence in Christian theology during or after the Reformation.[6]

In a cyclical model of history, all events are perceived as archetypal; one example of, say, the fall of an empire, will suffice as a model for all subsequent declining empires. But a linear model of history necessitated a different pedagogy. The easiest, if least efficient, literary response to this teleological perception of history was the unselective accumulation of recorded events in the form of annals. Such works operated on Orosius's theory that the shape of God's intention would manifest itself when sufficient information had been recorded; 'history demonstrated the workings of God's will on earth.'[7] Annals derived their inexhaustibly inclusive, paratactic form from Easter tables, the complex calendrical computations that were used in the Middle Ages to prognosticate liturgical observances.[8] But not everyone had the patience to wait for a pattern to emerge. And so theologians, on biblical authority, attempted to parcel history into significant 'ages of man.'[9] Kings caused history to be rewritten so as to trace a line of providence culminating in their reigns. Authors such as John Foxe saw history in terms of a significant minority, a 'saving remnant,' of the population. 'Such trends in historiography suggest a recognition that there was a great deal more to know about the past than medieval historians had assumed,'[10] and the pressures of growing nationalism as well as an increasing awareness of anachronism meant that the histories of the Tudor period, even the sweeping chronicle histories, were moving towards more consolidated narratives.[11] But whatever the pattern that was being 'discovered' in the events of history, there was a concern – so daunting to modern readers – with being comprehensive. But it was the broad overview, the accumulation of example, that was the proof of the posited pattern.

Boccaccio's *De casibus virorum illustrium* was one of the most influential versions of history the Renaissance produced. This fact has been consistently overlooked by even those few critics who have spent any time on *De casibus*. Traditionally the book is relegated to discussions of the history of tragedy. This is problematic for two reasons: first, while tragedy may be one of the most theorized of literary forms, it has attracted more vague thinking than any other literary form; second, the significant formal innovations of *De casibus* have nothing to do with tragedy.

As Henry Ansgar Kelly states in his eminently sensible book *Ideas and Forms of Tragedy from Aristotle to the Middle Ages*, 'the word "tragedy" is badly misused in most modern discussion of "the nature of tragedy," especially when dealing with dramatic forms.'[12] It is especially misused by those who draw upon Aristotle's *Poetics* for inspiration. Many twentieth-century critics have fallen into the same trap as their Italian Renaissance counterparts and treated the *Poetics* as a prescriptive, rather than a descriptive, treatise. Further, most critics focus on what Aristotle defines as the 'finest tragedy' and ignore his other descriptions. Finally, an emphasis on the 'spirit of tragedy,' especially in criticism of the first half of the twentieth century, has made much discussion of the form subjective to the point of mysticism.[13] What is needed is a simple, practical, working definition of tragedy. Kelly's solution is the one I shall adopt here: 'the name of tragedy is both a necessary and a sufficient condition for tragedy. That is, every work considered by its author to be a tragedy is a tragedy; and only those works considered by their authors to be tragedies are tragedies. As for works considered to be tragedies by other ancient or medieval writers ... they come under the category of ideas of tragedy rather than forms of tragedy.'[14]

With this definition in mind, what do we call *De casibus virorum illustrium*? What did Boccaccio consider the work? This is what he says in his introduction:

> To be sure, people who make a habit of sensuality are usually difficult to influence and are never swayed by the eloquence of history. Therefore I shall relate examples of what God or (speaking their own language) Fortune can teach them about those she raises up ...
>
> Therefore, from among the mighty I shall select the most famous, so when our princes see these rulers, old and spent, prostrated by the judgment of God, they will recognize God's power, the shiftiness of Fortune, and their own insecurity. They will learn the bounds of their merrymaking, and by the misfortunes of others, they can take counsel for their own profit.[15]

Boccaccio discusses fortune, he discusses the falls of rulers, but he does *not* use the word 'tragedy.' Boccaccio's interest in the falls of great men was based on the didactic potential of their historical examples. Boccaccio saw himself as a moral historian, not a tragedian. Indeed, for Boccaccio, and for most of the literate people of the Middle Ages, tragedy was a poorly understood, and clearly obsolete, dramatic form.[16] The very few times tragedy is mentioned in *De casibus* it is part of the historical context of the tale being told; Nero, for example, staged tragedies.

De casibus virorum illustrium, then, was written as history, not tragedy. What Boccaccio did was set out to prove that the mighty of the earth have always fallen. To do this he concatenated a huge number of annal-type biographies, biographies that had been chosen because they exhibited a specific plot line: *metabasis,* the reversal of situation from good to bad. *De casibus* combined this essentially satirical understanding of the individual life with the impetus in Christian historiography towards a broad teleological perception of history. It is not for the sake of prolixity that Boccaccio's work stretches from Adam to the immediate past of the author: it is the essential feature of its pedagogy. One biography, or a few, would not demonstrate that *metabasis* is the active principle in the history of humanity. Several hundred, however, do mount a compelling argument: 'as a constant flow of water will penetrate the hardest stone, so an adamantine heart is softened by a long narration' (48). It is for this reason that Boccaccio's title uses the plural.

Put another way, Boccaccio's work is neither allegorical nor typological; it is exemplary. Boccaccio was not suggesting historical parallels in his collection; he was mounting a comprehensive inductive argument about the shape of history in the exemplary mode. The rhetorical power of this mode was recognized as early as Gregory's *Dialogues;* 'Gregory remarks on several occasions that exempla touch the heart more directly than doctrine or rational argument,' especially the hearts of the 'uninstructed or the unconverted.'[17] But it is this mode that in part explains the lack of enthusiasm that modern readers feel for the work and its imitators. As J.A. Burrow explains,

> the exemplary mode is not very attractive to modern readers. We have been taught by so many good critics to respond sympathetically and intelligently to allegorical stories that the allegorical mode has once more become acceptable; but stories which represent themselves as 'examples,' whether in medieval or in Renaissance literature, are something of an embarrassment. There are good reasons for this. In a fiction which merely exemplifies an ethical concept ('patience,' 'gluttony') or an accepted truth ('Women are fickle,' *Radix malorum est cupiditas*), literature condemns itself to an ancillary role as the servant of the moral or political or religious beliefs of its age.[18]

Or, we should add, the historiographic.

The collection of sad stories exemplified one of the most prevalent medieval and Renaissance assumptions of the shape of history, that of universal decay. The theology of the post-lapsarian condition and the classical model of the four ages of man both seemed to support the notion that 'corruption is progressive, inevitable. It is both physical and moral: the world as it ages has become weaker and less fruitful, and people are more vicious now than in the past.'[19] So when Thomas Blundeville translated the Italian writers Francisco Patricio and Accontio Tridentino in his *The true order and Methode of wryting and reading Hystories* (1574), England's first historiographical study, his second point suggested the narrative form that he assumed history would manifest:

> And bycause euery thing hath hys beginning augmentacion, state, declinacion, and ende: The writer ought therfore to tell the things, so as therby a man may perceiue and discerne, that which apparteyneth to euery degree, and that, not onely as touching the Countrie or Citie: but also as touching the rule or dominion thereof. For the beginning, augmentacion, state, declynacion, and ende of a Countrie or Citie, and of the empire thereof, be not all one, but diuers things. (sig. A2r)

De casibus worked this macroscopic pattern out in the microcosm of the individual life, repeatedly demonstrating how the Fall had condemned humankind to 'naked poverty, anxious care, pallid disease, and sorrowing old age ... the instability of fortune; and with all these, the certain death of men' (4). As the world was in decline from Eden, as the Bronze Age was a poor successor of the Golden, so the individual, especially the rich and mighty, was fated to decline and die.

The *de casibus* form, then, if we define it by its original, is a type of history writing that brings together large numbers of biographies, all of which depict a life that moved from a good situation to a bad, with the purpose of demonstrating by the weight of the accumulated example that a falling pattern is typical of the lives of great persons. This form was followed closely by Boccaccio's successors in the tradition. Lydgate, in his second-hand translation of Boccaccio's work, extended that text chronologically, thereby adding more evidence to the argument. We have, between Boccaccio and Lydgate, a distilled example of this form in *The Monk's Tale* of Chaucer. The Monk gives a selective history of the world from Lucifer to Croesus and explains that he has a hundred such stories in his cell. Cumulatively the stories represent a vision of history in a highly condensed instance of the exemplary mode. In *Metrical Visions*, George Cavendish extended the *de casibus* formula into the history of his own lifetime, treating personal acquaintances such as Cardinal Wolsey, Henry VIII, and Anne Boleyn.

The *de casibus* form should be distinguished from the *Fürstenspiegel*, the 'Mirror for Princes.' The latter is a text of counsel, intended for a ruler, often written in the exemplary mode. A *de casibus* can be a *Fürstenspiegel* – *Fall of Princes* clearly is – but a *Fürstenspiegel* is not *de casibus* unless it concatenates biographies to demonstrate a historical teleology. Allan H. Gilbert estimates that, between 800 and 1700, Europe produced some 1,000 conduct books for monarchs, but very few of them are in the *de casibus* format.[20] For example, John of Salisbury's *Policratus* (1159) makes extensive use of exempla, but his stories are 'oriented to the demonstration of how abstract principles of moral and political behaviour may be employed in everyday life.'[21] Similarly, Hoccleve's *The Regement of Princes* is a *Fürstenspiegel* written for Prince Henry, later Henry V, that uses historical exempla to counsel the prince in such virtues as dignity, justice, and honesty, but it is not a *de casibus* work for it offers no vision of history.[22]

The *Mirror* was to have been a chronological extension of Lydgate's book included in an edition of *Fall of Princes*. As Lydgate extended Boccaccio, so Baldwin et al. were to have extended Lydgate, tracing the pattern of rise and fall into the realm of British history. Indeed, as the printing history of the *Mirror* itself demonstrates, the text expanded outwards towards the chronological perimeters of British history. The edition of 1559 was concerned with the Wars of the Roses. Subsequent editions under Baldwin's editorship added tragedies up unto the life of Cardinal Wolsey. The first of the independent editors, John Higgins, concentrated on the period from Brute to the reign of Caesar. The next editor, Thomas Blennerhasset, applauded Higgins's efforts but deplored the spottiness of the overall chronology: 'Doo you not consider, that al the fine wyts that England hath inioyed these many yeres, haue busied their braynes very much, to make an English *Mirrour for Magistrates*, which booke is left euen vnto this day, like the vnperformed image of *Venus*, paynted by *Apelles*?' (2: 380). He attempted a partial reparation by describing the period from the Roman Conquest to the time of William the Conqueror. Richard Niccols, the final editor, did some historical patchwork and added 'England's Eliza.' The totality of the text, when the individual stories are arranged according to their historical chronology, as they are in Haslewood's edition of 1815, represents a rough summation of

British history from Brute to Elizabeth told in just under a hundred poems.[23]

The evolution of the *Mirror* text, then, was a manifestation of the *de casibus* impetus towards a broad overview of history and the pedagogy based on data accumulation that such entails. The authors were also conscious that they were working in a form that was ruled by the dictates of historiography. When one of Baldwin's collaborators demanded to hear a story out of chronological order, Baldwin corrected him: 'Nay soft ... we wyl take the cronycles, & note theyr places, & as they cum, so wil we orderly reade them al' (1: 244–5). Many of the prose links in the Baldwin editions contain queries over the accuracy of specific details (see, for example, 1: 110). Higgins's justification for his edition was as much historiographical as it was poetic. He felt that the chroniclers had been remiss in not elaborating on the earliest British history (2: 35–8). Blennerhasset, in the preface to his edition, apologized that he did not have more historical texts at hand with which to check his references, but he dutifully listed his major sources (2: 381). Niccols was similarly reassuring: 'not taking a poeticall licence to fashion all things after mine owne fancie, but limiting my selfe within the bounds of an historicall writer, I haue followed those authors, who in the censure of our best iudgements are most authenticall' (2: 545).

Not only did the authors of the *Mirror* display an awareness of the criterion of historical accuracy, but they were very conscious that they are correcting the slovenliness of previous chroniclers, who were insufficiently specific in delineating the teleology inherent in their material:

> Vnfruytfull Fabyan folowed the face
> Of time and dedes, but let the causes slip:
> Whych Hall hath added, but with double grace,
> For feare I thinke least trouble might him trip:
> For this or that (sayeth he) he felt the whip.
> Thus story writers leave the causes out,
> Or so rehears them, as they wer in doubt.

> But seing causes are the chiefest thinges
> That should be noted of the story wryters,
> That men may learne what endes al causes bringes
> They be vnwurthy the name of Croniclers,
> That leave them cleane out of their registers.

Or doubtfully report them: for the fruite
Of reading stories, standeth in the suite.

(John, Earl of Worcester, 1: 198)

Here Baldwin seems to be anticipating the criticism of the historian
that Sir Philip Sidney levelled in his *Defence of Poesie*: that he 'is so tied,
not to what should be, but to what is, to the particular truth of things,
and not to the general reason of things, that his example draweth no
necessarie consequence, and therefore a lesse fruitfull doctrine.'[24] For
Baldwin, as for Boccaccio, the accumulation of the particular truth
of things would, through induction, manifest the general reason of
things. There might, occasionally, be exceptions to the rule, but they
would be insufficient to undermine the teleology attested to by the
vast weight of historical exempla. *A Mirror for Magistrates*, then, and
other *de casibus* works, offered a fruitful doctrine, the vision of providentially ordered history, by drawing attention to the necessary consequences of myriad examples. It is no wonder that Sidney approved of
this history book.[25]

To further understand the popularity and significance of the *Mirror*,
we must see it in relation to specific Elizabethan concepts of history.
Indeed, the evolution of the *Mirror* was intertwined with the evolution
in English historiography from 1550 to the early 1600s. History
throughout this period was seen as a form of instruction; 'the chief criterion for historical truth was moral utility.'[26] History was regarded as
second only to Scripture for teaching morality, and it was therefore
very popular with the middle class and educators.[27] Chronicle histories, both of England and of London, were popular throughout the
Elizabethan period,[28] and Ralegh's *History of the World* would outsell
Shakespeare's *Folio*.[29] 'All history, and especially political narrative,
aimed at giving advice, however subtly and obliquely.'[30] But ideas of
history changed during this period. This change was not steady or
regular, but, in broad terms, we may argue that early sixteenth-
century history emphasized the first causes of events, the intervention
of God into history. Late sixteenth-century history, under the influence of Guicciardini, Machiavelli, and Bodin, became concerned with
second causes, with the intervention of men into history.[31] By the
early seventeenth century, the lessons sought in history were increasingly secular and public. These new histories emphasized political
wisdom and practical, not moral, lessons.[32] The classical historian

most often imitated was no longer Livy, but, rather, Tacitus, whose axiomatic writing style lent itself to pragmatic aphorisms.[33] And, at the same time, 'the creation of the Tudor dynasty, founded on doubtful historical claims, motivated both government and politically astute subjects to become aware of history as a branch of knowledge that could be manipulated for ideological purposes. Such manipulation was made possible not least by a growing awareness of historiography as a methodologically eclectic and *under*determined practice.'[34] History, for some writers at least, was recognized as constructed, not merely recorded, and the principles of that construction were beginning to be acknowledged as determined by specific political agendas rather than immutable truths.

As we have seen, all of the *Mirror* editors purported to follow the discipline of contemporary historiography, and the early editions of the *Mirror* did accord with trends in history writing: they traced providence through a selective editing of the chronicles organized around the narrative of individual lives. But while late sixteenth-century history writing went on to emphasize the will and character of men and their ability to shape events, the later editions of the *Mirror* became more, not less, concerned with providence. They increasingly traced a mechanistic teleology shaped around moral turpitude, not political will; they increasingly promulgated an unmediated version of Tudor history and, later, Tudor nostalgia. In short, the *Mirror* evolved away from the historiography it claimed as authority. Put another way, it retreated from the capacity that textual authority, especially the authority of historical exempla, had to challenge political power. This evolution can be traced through details of the *Mirror* texts: the chronologies of the tragedies, the dedications of the four main editions, and the framing devices that each editor employed.

To reiterate, the first *Mirror*, edited by Baldwin, contains tragedies that roughly covered the period of the Wars of the Roses. Subsequent Baldwin editions took the chronology up to the time of Wolsey. The next editor, Higgins, filled in the period from Brute until Caesar. The third editor, Blennerhasset, covered the time from the Roman Conquest until William the Conqueror. The final editor, Niccols, filled in gaps and added a poem in praise of Queen Elizabeth.

The choices of these chronological perimeters are suggestive. Baldwin chose a period of unrest, civil war, on the brink of the Reformation. The choice was overtly political and led to the *Mirror* being suppressed during the reign of Mary. Baldwin's explanation of the restriction process, offered some years later, is cryptic: 'The wurke was begun, & part of it printed .iiii. yeare agoe, but hyndred by the Lord Chauncellour that then was, nevertheles, through the meanes of my lord Stafford, lately perused & licenced' (1: 66). Why was the Lord Chancellor, Stephen Gardiner, Bishop of Winchester, concerned? There was one obvious reason for the suppression of the text: several of the stories in the book directly, or through analogy and allusion, referred to Edward Seymour, the Protector of England during the youth of Edward VI. Seymour is treated in the *Mirror* not as a proud nobleman felled by fortune, but rather as one punished for virtue.[35] Baldwin and his fellows, through the example of this Protestant zealot, were analysing the role of the protectorate and, perhaps, advocating an extremist Protestant policy for contemporary England. Another reason for suppression was the tragedy entitled 'The fall of Robert Tresilian chiefe Justice of Englande ... for misconstruying the lawes, and expounding them to serve the Princes affections' (1: 73). It seemed a clear allusion to the recent trial of Sir Nicholas Throckmorton for Protestant sedition.[36]

But there may have been a more general reason for the suppression of this book: the vast majority of the tales in the editions of the *Mirror* put together under Baldwin's supervision castigate political failings; 'tyranny, treason, rebellion, dishonest flattery of princes – these are the sins against the public weale which are recorded in the *Mirror*.'[37] For the *Mirror* contributors, it seems, the past should not, perhaps could not, be separated from the practical and political concerns of the present, and this was something that the government of Queen Mary was not interested in being told, especially through as prestigious a book as the *De casibus*, a work generally regarded as a text of political instruction.[38] Or, as Larry Scanlon explains,

> to a society where an expanding ruling class was converting more and more of its customary hegemony into statute law and textually recorded administrative procedure, and where the most administratively advanced monarchy in Europe was becoming an increasing locus of ideological contention, the *De casibus* projected an image of authority that was public and textual, yet also exclusive, that offered a share of such authority to all who could read it, yet reassured its readers that such shares remain the exclusive property of those above the *vulgus*.[39]

We might expect this from the very title of the book. Although he was supposed to be writing a supplement to Lydgate's *Fall of Princes*, Baldwin chose to ignore the title of that work and, therefore, separate his book from a 'fall' tradition begun by Boccaccio. 'Mirror' titles had been popular in antiquity, and then again starting in the eleventh century, especially in Continental Latin literature.[40] Although they had been a constant, though minor, tradition in English literature, it was only after the publication of *A Mirror for Magistrates* that 'mirror' titles become a true vogue in England, peaking in the early seventeenth century.[41] Baldwin, in making this shift in the name, was directing the reader towards the book's didactic potential. While *Fall of Princes* suggested tragedy, declaring its narrative arc in its title, the *Mirror* did not. 'Fall' suggested empathy would be required of the reader; 'mirror' did not. One looks in a mirror not to study the remote and pathetic past, but for information about oneself. As this book was 'a mirror' for magistrates, it was to be a tool for self-inspection for the powerful; as its focus was historical and political, it was directing the powerful to study their own fates in those of their immediate, and conspicuously unsuccessful, predecessors.

It is strange, then, there remains a contemporary critical tendency to dismiss the book as politically conservative.[42] The critics who do so seem to be fixated on those passages in the *Mirror*, primarily to be found in the prose links, that articulate a faith in the absolutist hereditary monarchy. For example, after the tragedy of the Blacksmith, Baldwin says to his collaborators: 'The matter is notable to teach all people as well offycers as subiectes to consyder their estates and to lyue in loue and obedience to the hygheste powers, whatsoeuer they be, whom god eyther by byrth, lawe, succession, or vniuersal eleccion, doth or shall aucthorise in his owne roume to execute his lawes & iustice, amonge any people or nacyon: For by all these meanes God placeth his deputies' (1: 419). Baldwin rationalizes this panegyric on the divine right of kings: 'The frantyke heades whiche disable our Queene, because she is a woman, and our kynge because he is a straunger, to be our princes and chiefe gouernors, hath cause me to saye thus much' (1: 420). Baldwin is praising Queen Mary even though he could not have favoured her Catholic policies or her marriage to Philip II of Spain. This is not political hypocrisy or sycophancy. Rather, it is mid-sixteenth-century patriotism, a patriotism that was focused, above all, on the person of the monarch. Over the next thirty years, many of England's thinkers and writers would construct a sense of nationality that transcended the individual person of the monarch, but it was not in place in the 1550s.[43] So though Baldwin was attacking the Marian resistance, he should not be considered a simple-minded apologist for Mary's policies or Tudor absolutism (that charge may more justly be levelled at the *Mirror* editors who succeeded him). To a large degree, those were beside the point. The political radicalism of the *Mirror* lay in its use of history and its choice of audience. Baldwin and his fellow citizen collaborators were targeting the corruption of magistrates, attempting to force their social superiors into an acknowledgment of the consequences of their actions to the public weal. Given the institutional corruption that spread during the reigns of Edward and Mary, this was much more than a theoretical exercise, and the *Mirror*'s suppression is proof of its potential efficacy.[44] The legitimate monarch was irrelevant to this discussion; she was literally God-given. But all others who possessed political agency were being asked to view their actions in the *Mirror*, a surface that reflected all the more sharply for being composed from the lives of the recently deceased. If the *Mirror* contributed directly to the formation of the idea of nation, it was with these two concepts: that the powerful who implement the will of the land are separate from both the land and the monarch, and recent history must delimit the consciousness of the politically enfranchised.

These were not concepts that the subsequent editors of the *Mirror* mastered. So Higgins, in his edition, jumped back in time to Albanact, the son of the Trojan Brutus, and the material he covered was the legend of *The Brut*, that mythical period of British history first detailed by Geoffrey of Monmouth and elaborated upon by patriots and poets into the early eighteenth century.[45] His purpose in focusing on this ancient time was 'to fetch our Histories from the beginning, & make them as ample as the Chronicles of any other Country or Nation' (2: 35). In doing so he was emulating the earlier chroniclers who sought to construct a prehistory for Britain that accorded with the familiar and heroic tradition of classical epic literature, but he was also reacting against contemporary trends in English historiography.[46] *The Brut*, and to a lesser degree the Arthur legend, was under attack in the late sixteenth century. Historians who questioned these myths included Polydore Vergil, Robert Fabyan, John Rastell, John Twyne, George Lilly, Thomas Cooper, and William Camden. Even Edmund Spenser dismissed the Trojan origins of England as invention.[47] The legends had their defenders, most notably John Leland, Sir John Price – both of whom attacked Polydore Vergil in print – and Holinshed, but they were a vocal minority.

Indeed, as Arthur B. Ferguson has demonstrated, mythology itself, rather than its putative historical content, became a subject of historical study in the late Elizabethan period. 'Placing mythopoeic process within the context of historical time meant, of course, accepting the limitations inherent in any attempt to organize prehistory,' and it opened the door for a re-examination of British patriotic myths such as *The Brut* and the Arthur stories.[48] And the very process of rethinking the national prehistory led to fascinating work on the origins of English peoples and to some inspired guesses: John Twyne suggested that the island of Britain had once been joined by a land bridge to the Continent. Eventually, the emergence of an evolutionary notion of civilization, a theory that may have grown out of Augustine's famous comparison of the life history of the race with that of the individual, was postulated. This broad and progressive theory (that was mitigated, of course, by the notion of universal decline from the Fall), which Ferguson calls the 'cave myth,' postulated a view of humankind moving from a primitive early stage, in which people lived in child-like savagery in caves, to the contemporary, mature dignity of European civilization.[49] Proponents of this theory found exciting evidence in the primitive societies of the New World and Ireland.

Higgins, then, in reciting tragedies from legendary prehistory was retreating from the concerns of current historiography into something much, much safer: patriotic legend, quasi-mythical events so distant in time and entrenched in tradition that they could not be construed as having contemporary political or historiographic significance. The titles of Higgins's biographies proclaim their folk-tale morality:

Kimarus shewes howe for his euill life he was deuoured by wilde beastes

Elstride the concubine of Locrinus myserably drowned by Gwendoline his wyfe, declares her presumption, lewde life and infortunate fall

Mempricius giuen all to luste, pleasure and the sinne of Sodomye: telles how he was deuoured of wolues

(2: 180, 87, 124)

There was little danger the Elizabethan magistrate would see himself reflected in these mirrors, and that fact undermined the exemplary mode which gave the *de casibus* tradition its rhetorical power.

For the exemplum's enactment of authority in fact assumes a process of identification on the part of its audience. That is to say, the exemplum

expects the members of its audience to be convinced by its *sententia* pre-
cisely because it expects them to put themselves in the position of its protagonists, to emulate the protagonist's moral success, or avoid his or her
moral failure. It persuades by conveying a sense of communal identity
with its moral lesson.[50]

Further, a good number of Higgins's histories have nothing at all to do
with British history. His inclusion of a story of Julius Caesar can be
rationalized because Caesar 'first made this Realme tributary to the
Romaynes' (2: 290), but the inclusion of the emperors Tiberius and
Caligula cannot be so justified, and Higgins does not attempt to do
so.[51] Higgins's retreat from the immediate past came just as English
historians were increasingly realizing its importance in their studies,
an awareness that would peak during the Civil War and Restoration.[52]
More broadly, this retreat took the *Mirror* out of the process of patriotic
self-definition that directed so much of the intellectual energy of the
late Tudor period, a process that entailed a spurning of universal history in favour of the national and dynastic. Higgins seemed bent on
making the *Mirror* a book of sweeping antiquarian lore rather than
English political history.

Blennerhasset, the third *Mirror* editor, covered that part of ancient
and legendary history from the rebellion against the Romans up to the
historical Harold I. He did not deal with King Arthur, but he offered
tragedies of Vortiger, Uther Pendragon, Queen Hellina (the British
mother of Constantine the Great), and Cadwallader, the last of the
Briton monarchs. Although he did cover some historical figures, all of
his characters were sufficiently distant historically to be politically
neutral. Blennerhasset did, however, have pretensions to didacticism,
and many of his titles point to obvious lessons. The subtitle for the
tragedy of Sigebert reads: 'This Tragedie dooth teach both Prince and
subiect his duetie at large' (2: 452); the message, however, is aimed primarily at the subject and emphasizes the unimpeachable sanctity of
authority, for 'he who doth resist the Magistrate, / Resisteth god' (2:
461). Most of the lessons are less political. As the title of the tragedy of
Pendragon explains, 'this example is most necessary for the present
time' (2: 435). Blennerhasset does not, however, attack political inepti-
tude as personified by Pendragon; rather, he attacks contemporary
British womanhood because 'all voyde of veyless ... [they] runne /
And rome about at euerye feast and playe, / They wanderyng walke in
euery streete and way' (2: 439). Blennerhasset was worried about lust,

and a disproportionate number of the stories he chooses to recite teach its perils.

Niccols, the final editor, retreated into myth, Stuart propaganda, and Tudor nostalgia. He opened, tellingly, with the Arthur legend. Although persistent in poetic treatments throughout the seventeenth century, the Arthur myth had come under attack by various historians in the late sixteenth century; it had been scrutinized since at least the time of Caxton.[53] Under James, the attack on Arthur took on a political dimension. James claimed a dual lineage (both Tudor and Stuart) from Arthur, and proposed to fulfil Merlin's prophecy of a united Great Britain by wearing the crowns of both Scotland and England.[54] The early years of James's reign were the cause of much genealogical and historical research supporting the idea of a 'Great Britain,' a unified England and Scotland ruled from London. By the time of Niccols's edition of the *Mirror*, however, there was renewed controversy over the historicity of the Arthur myth. Historians attacked the Arthur myth, and therefore James's mythic trappings, by questioning the historical reliability of Geoffrey of Monmouth, the Arthur authority,[55] while amateur genealogists such as the parson George Owen Harry argued James's reign was fulfilling the prophecy of Cadwallader himself.[56] Niccols's version, appearing in a work that purported to be primarily historical – it invoked the muse Clio, not Melpomene – reasserted the stock Tudor version of the Arthur story, giving a sentimental and patriotic rendering of the tale that differed significantly from Geoffrey's only in its vehement denial of Arthur's illegitimacy (564).

We should also note that, in the edition that Niccols assembled, he chose to leave out certain of the tragedies that were written before him. Notably, he left out the tragedies of James I, James IV, and the battle of Flodden, all of which might cause offence to the Scottish king.[57] The other characters he treated, such as Richard III and Edward II, comprised the standard rogues' gallery of Tudor myth. The final celebratory poem, 'England's Eliza,' gave up all pretence of being a critical mirror or a tragedy. It is a patriotic, comic, popular history of Elizabeth. Seemingly trying to prove Roy Strong's adage that 'for the Stuarts all roads finally led back to Elizabeth,'[58] Niccols laments the passing of not only the queen, but Edmund Spenser, 'that Fairie Queenes sweet singer ... That to the dead eternitie could giue' (779).

Baldwin's editions were dedicated to the magistrates of the land, 'to the nobilitye and all other in office' (1: 63). Though 'magistrate' was often used as a synonym for 'justice of the peace,' it also meant 'any civil officer charged with the administration of the laws [or] member of the executive government' (*Oxford English Dictionary*), noble or not. At the very least, Baldwin and his colleagues were directing their attention to high civic authorities – 'common councilmen, hospital officers, auditors ... bridgemasters, chamberlains, aldermen, sheriffs, and mayors'[59] – but probably also those more highly placed bureaucrats and nobility who surrounded and advised the Queen. Baldwin complimented his intended readership and acknowledged their power and prestige: 'ye be all Gods, as many as have in your charge any ministracion of Iustice' (1: 65). This is not merely epideictic convention; Baldwin emphasized the responsibility attendant upon power and posited the broad political implications of magisterial corruption: 'the goodnes or badnes of any realme lyeth in the goodnes or badnes of the rulers' (1: 64). To insure the goodness of the ruling class, and hence the soundness of the realm, Baldwin offered the *Mirror* as cure for the diseased and prophylactic for the sound. It functioned by demonstrating how God shall 'plage such shameles presumption and hipocrisy, and that with shamefull death, diseases, or infamy' (1: 65) by proving inevitable divine retribution: 'For here as in a loking glas, you shall see (if any vice be in you) howe the like hath bene punished in other heretofore, whereby admonished, I trust it will be a good occasion to move you to the soner amendment' (1: 65–6).

Baldwin and his colleagues, then, conceived of a privileged readership for their work. So confident were they of this readership that many of the issues they raised were handled with an eye to upper-class entitlement. A disagreement in their chronicle sources over a question of blood relation leads to this caveat:

> This disagreynge of wryters is a great hinderaunce of the truthe, & no small cumbrauns to such as be diligent readers, besides the harme that may happen in succession of herytages. It were therfore a wurthye and a good dede for the nobilytie, to cause al the recordes to be sought, & a true and prefecte cronicle therout to be wrytten. vnto which we refer the decydyng of this, & of all other lyke controversies, gevyng this to vnderstand in the mean tyme, That no man shall thinke his title eyther better or wurse by any thing that it wrytten in any part of thys treatyse. For the onlye thynge which is purposed herin, is by example of others miseries, to diswade all men from all sinnes and vices. (1: 267)

They also hoped that their audience would be learned. In the prose link after the story of Lord Hastings, one of the contributors complains that the story was 'very darke, and hard to be vnderstood': 'I like it the better (quoth an other.) For that shal cause it to be the oftener reade, and the better remembred. Considering also that it is written for the learned (for such all Magistrates are or should be) it can not be to hard, so long as it is sound and learnedly wrytten' (1: 297).

The teleology implicit in accumulated historical example, then, was to motivate the magistrate to good management of the realm. Baldwin admitted that history occasionally afforded examples of good men killed for their virtue, but he warned his readers to nevertheless 'cease not you to be vertuous, but do your offices to the vttermost' for God shall guarantee 'eternal glory both here and in heaven' (1: 67). The eternal glory of 'here' was the fame of an honourable name; Baldwin was playing to the concern for honour and reputation that was the prime motivator of local officeholders in Tudor and Stuart England.[60] Baldwin's dedication, then, was didactic, offered a teleological reading of history to political ends, and played to the immediate concerns of its specialized, educated readership. This dedication clearly marked the book as a *Fürstenspiegel*, a 'Mirror for Princes,' but with a difference: it addressed authority below the prince, making it a sort of 'Mirror for Bureaucrats.' It was aimed at the audience that it could most realistically expect to impact, increasing its potential efficacy by targeting the largest, if not the most glamorous, portion of the Elizabethan power structure.

This fact also marks the Baldwin editions of the *Mirror* as a relative of the courtesy book as well as the *Fürstenspiegel*. These books, epitomized but by no means exhausted in England by Thomas Hoby's 1561 translation of Baldasare Castiglione's *Il Cortegiano* (1528), were practical self-help books that 'convert[ed] the tools of rule, of domination and self-determination, into a commodity packaged for the open market of the literate.'[61] Putatively aimed at an exclusive, entitled readership, and often framed in elaborate conceits of fictionality, the courtesy books did not merely find an audience with a social elite that was attempting to construct a rhetoric of self-worth, but also were snapped up by the upwardly mobile as how-to books for the social graces of privilege. Or, as Frank Whigham has put it, 'the advent of widespread social mobility stimulated the established members of the aristocracy to conduct, as if for the first time, a rhetorical defense of their exclusive right to power and privilege. They mustered a complex array of ideological maneuvers, many of which were soon co-opted by the mobile.'[62] The pretence of fictionality, a rhetorical move that ensured the books did not give political offence or appear to be too vulgarly practical, was often supplemented with stories of long-lost chivalric heroes and traditions. So, a book like William Segar's *Honor, Military and Civil* (1602) argued for the historical veracity of King Arthur and intermingled his adventures with those of the more recent heroes such as Sir Francis Drake in the pursuit of its arguments regarding chivalric ritual and symbol.[63] When such historical or quasi-historical examples were employed, they were, almost inevitably, positive and romantic: chivalric knights, the flowers of courtesy, were held up as models to emulate.

The *Mirror*, and *de casibus* literature in general, worked the opposite way, as a sort of inverted courtesy book. It rejected any pretence of fictionality, not only insisting upon the historical veracity of its accounts, but overpowering any resistance to the example of history through sheer bulk of precedent. The stories related were overwhelmingly negative, and so *de casibus* literature acted as a sombre antidote to romantic pretence. The Baldwin editions of the *Mirror* also cut through the polite fiction of the readers' class exclusivity. Dedicated to magistrates, those at the edge of court life who have chosen to serve the state, these books focused on a readership that was privileged but not necessarily entitled. This was exactly the same market that bought courtesy books in an attempt to learn the techniques of self-definition necessary to make the final leap into nobility, or at least the class culture of nobility. Baldwin's dedication, then, alerts us to the subversive cultural positioning of the *Mirror*: reversing the tropes of courtesy literature, the book sought to force into political and moral introspection that portion of the populace that wielded power, but craved title.

Higgins reiterated the title of Baldwin's dedication, directing his introductory remarks to 'the nobilitie and all other in office' (2: 31), but whereas the Baldwin dedication then asks that 'God graunt wisedome' (1: 63), Higgins continues: 'God graunt the increase of wysedome.' Higgins, then, flatters his readership, attributing to them a native wisdom (all magistrates *should* be learned) that Baldwin does not assume they have. Later in the dedication, Higgins proclaimed that he would not repeat 'which Maister Baldwin hath so learnedly touched in his Epistle of the other volume of this booke' (2: 34), and indeed he does not. He does not, for example, urge his readers to look into the *Mirror* to see their own faults reflected. Rather, he argues through classical, not English, example that the great figures of history fell from grace

'for wante of temperance' (2: 32). To temperance he adds 'three other
Cardinall vertues whiche are requisite in him that should be in author-
itie: that is to saye, Prudence, Iustice, and Fortitude, which so beauti-
fully adorne and beautife all estates' (2: 32). We should note several
things here: Higgins used classical examples sufficiently distant from
English politics that generalizations about them were relatively safe.
Second, the virtues of temperance and prudence that Higgins extolled
were more frequently associated with the citizenry than with the ruling nobility. Third, in Higgins's formulation these virtues adorn 'all
estates' and he describes the *Mirror* as being 'full of fitte instructions
for preseruation of eche estate' (2: 36). He even reinterprets Baldwin's
editions to make them more class inclusive:

> Examples there for all estates you finde,
> For iudge (I say) what iustice he should vse:
> The noble man to beare a noble mynde,
> And not him selfe ambiciously abuse:
> The Gentlemen vngentlenes refuse:
> The ryche, and poore: and euery one may see,
> Which way to loue and lyve in his degree.   (2: 41)

We might argue that this is indicative of an attempt to extend the
authority of historical exempla to the general public, were not those
exempla so distant and denuded of political import. Higgins simply
had his eye on a much less specialized readership than did Baldwin.

Blennerhasset's edition had no formal dedication because it was
published without the author's permission. Instead, the printer, the
singularly unsuccessful Richard Webster, appended a letter to the
'friendly Reader' rationalizing the circumstances of the printing and
introducing a letter by Blennerhasset written from his military outpost.
In it Blennerhasset explains how he intended to fill in the gaps in the
Mirror's chronology. The closest he comes to a dedication is his praise
for his commander, Thomas Leighton, whom he believed embodied
the best of Constantine the Great, Licurgus, Solon, and Epaminundas
(2: 382).[64] This is not a formal dedication, but it does seem to be leading
towards that which appeared in the last version of the *Mirror*.

Niccols dedicated his edition to Lord Charles Howard, the Earl of
Nottingham, with an introductory verse that was a banal and sycophantic plea for patronage. Complimenting Howard on his military
achievements, Niccols goes on and

Most humblie craues your lordly Lions aid
Gainst monster Enuie, while she tels her storie
Of Britaine Princes, and that royall Maid,
In whose chaste hymne her *Clio* sings your glorie.   ([551])

Instead of displaying a critical mirror to a flawed magistrate, Niccols
begs his favour. He presumed that his subject material would *not* be
read as reflecting upon its titular reader, that the material was safe,
apolitical, and quaint. If Howard, to whom some fifty publications
were dedicated in his life,[65] favoured the book, Niccols promised 'my
Muse shall frame / Mirrours more worthie your renowned name'
([551]). There is no sense here that historical authority will, or can,
impinge upon class or political prestige. Howard was not a magistrate
to be swayed by the weight of exempla; he was a nobleman to be enter-
tained with a collection of reassuringly familiar biographies that cul-
minated in a comic vision of the reign of Elizabeth. The mirror had
become a portrait, an antiquarian curio.[66]

The stories in each edition are introduced and framed by a prose or
poetic device, and each frame presents a figure who guides the poet or
poets through the history, a person to whom the ghosts make their
complaints. The Baldwin editions are framed by prose notes explaining in detail the events surrounding the publication of the *Mirror*.
Between the individual biographies, Baldwin recorded the comments
of the assembled writers on the stories they have heard. The frame,
then, is a realistic prose recounting of the trials of multiple authorship,
and the discussion is eclectic. The assembled readers discuss everything from the veracity of their sources to the theological implications
of the depiction of the underworld: 'it sauoreth so much of Purgatory,
whiche the papistes haue digged thereout, that the ignorant maye
therby be deceyued' (2: 346). Baldwin did this sort of self-conscious
explication elsewhere, most notably in *Beware the Cat* (1584).[67] In the
Baldwin editions the guide figure is Baldwin himself.

Higgins's framing device was a poem relating a dream vision. The
narrator, on a sad winter's night, falls asleep while reading a copy of *A
Mirror for Magistrates*. In his sleep he is introduced to 'men mighty
bigge, in playne and straunge atyre' (2: 44) who repeat their stories to
him. Higgins took the *Mirror* back to Lydgate and the hoary tradition
of the dream frame.[68] The stories of the book, then, were encapsulated
by a device that proclaimed their artifice. They were poems first, his-

tory second. In his dream frame, Higgins is assigned the guide Morpheus. Morpheus is ordered by Somnus to 'shewe ... from the first to th'ende, / Such persons as in Britayne Fortune thralde' (2: 43). Morpheus leads the poet to a hall, and there acts as a stage manager, directing the ghosts of past heroes to tell 'Their names, and lyues: their haps, and haples days: / And by what meanes from Fortunes globe they fel' (2: 45). He reappears in the links between stories, but only as an introducer.

Blennerhasset's frame was a short allegorical induction, but it does not feature the poet; rather, the characters of Inquisition and Memory set about the task of repairing the gaps in the previous editions of the *Mirror*. While they offer some speculation on the tales – 'It was a great pitie ... that thys man [Guidericus] liued in the tyme of blinde ignorance, when neyther vertue, nor religion were knowen' (2: 398) – they let the stories and their obviously moralistic titles carry the weight of explication. So divorced are they from political didacticism that they fill one entire introduction with a discussion of English poetic meter (2: 450).

Niccols returned to the safety of the dream frame. His edition was entitled *A Winter Nights Vision*, and it begins with a long poem that attempts to recapture the pathetic fallacy of the most famous poem in the *Mirror*, Sackville's 'Induction,' which appeared in the 1563 edition. Niccols's guide is Memory, aided by Fame, whose job it is to

> summon up the ghosts of all those worthie men,
> That mong'st our Mirrours are not found, that each one orderly
> May come to thee, to tell the truth of his sad tragedie.   (560)

Memory's mission is to keep

> the wealthie store
> Of times rich treasure, where the deeds that haue been done of yore
> I do record, and when in bookes I chance to find the Fame
> Of any after death decai'd, I do reuiue the same.   (559)

Memory's comments between stories are almost entirely recountings of historical circumstances surrounding the preceding or upcoming narrative. Editorializing is rendered unnecessary by the heavy-handed moral rhetoric of the tales themselves.

We can, then, trace several progressions. The text moved from a historical period that had immediate political implications for the present to areas that were distant and legendary. Its pointed didactic dedication aimed at the elevated readership it meant to educate became a sycophantic plea for patronage from a higher class. Its realistic frame detailing the historical and didactic intentions of the authors became a 'winter night's vision,' a doggerel introductory device that, whatever the author's protestations, identified what followed as poetry, not history. In short, the text metamorphosed from an ideologically aware poetic history into a sentimental historical poem.

There are other ways we may describe the progress of the *Mirror* through its editions and editors. The original book was polyvocal; it contains not only the voices of the contributors, recorded in the prose links and giving testament to the communal effort of the production, but also the voices of different ghosts, each articulating the moral of its own exemplum. Because the various monologues were written by different members of the writers' collective, they offered a wide variety of styles and tones within the restrictive *de casibus* format. And because the monologues of the ghosts are framed by the prose links that detail the process of composition, the historical exempla are always contextualized in the immediate present; past and present permeate each other. This double community of voices – authors and ghosts – a radical heteroglossia, addressed itself to another community, that of magistrates, the bureaucrats of the emergent Elizabethan state, inviting them to view themselves in the latter, but perhaps also the former. For as a group of learned citizens studying the chronicles for precedent and pattern, Baldwin and his collaborators were themselves roughly analogous to the magistrates in their endeavours. The mirror, then, is a double one; the magistrate might see himself reflected in history (the ghosts) or historiography (the authors), in record or the interpretation of record. In either reflection the range of voices prohibited the easy dismissal of the text as singular and, therefore, eccentric.[69]

This should remind us, again, of courtesy literature. *The Courtier* was written as a dialogue in imitation of classical precedent and in accord with contemporaneous Italian fashion.[70] Many of its imitators followed suit. This form provided at least two functions. First, it allowed the authors to engage with a variety of conflicting definitions and opinions upon the questions of courtesy and courtliness, an engagement that was all the more necessary because shifts in social structure and the rise of the bureaucratic function were creating new dynamics of social definition that brought conflicting notions of entitlement together. This formal acknowledgment of conflict demonstrated an awareness by the authors of the ideological nature of courtesy, courtliness, and, by extension, class itself. Second, as Frank Whigham has noted, 'the numerous dialogues show interlocutors doing with the text's agenda just what the reader will do with it; just as Fregoso, say, might quote Aristotle incrementally, for different purposes on different occasions, so may the reader quote Castiglione, ad hoc.'[71] Similarly, the *Mirror*, in its prose links, offered varied and sometimes conflicting authorial dialogue on the historical record, drawing attention to its ideological import. And the links do with history what the reader will do with the *Mirror*: imagine it, dramatize it, discuss it, and evaluate its implications for the present.[72]

But by the time we get to Niccols, this polyvocal engagement with history is lost. Niccols was a single writer, whose monologues all manifest a flatness of voice that comes from their heavy-handed reiteration of the historical caricatures of the Tudor myth, addressing himself to a single potential patron. That man, Charles Howard, Earl of Nottingham, first cousin once removed to the Queen, Lord High Admiral, member of the Privy Council, was a man of great privilege who, at the age of seventy-four (in the year Niccols's edition was printed), was not likely to be swayed one way or another in his enactment of public policy by the authority of distant and legendary history. Nor, as we have seen, did Niccols expect him to be. The heteroglossia of the *Mirror* had been replaced by univocality and epideictic supplication.

Further, Niccols ended the *Mirror* tradition with 'England's Eliza,' a comic poem that recites the deeds of Elizabeth's reign in the third person. This breaks the exemplary mode of the *de casibus* by offering a story that does not fit the dominant idea, here historiographical, or form, monologue, of the collection. It also denuded it of the authority of identification. No magistrate or nobleman could presume to put himself in the position of Elizabeth I. Her position in history, or rather as the culmination of history, a position enforced by the Jacobean nostalgia for the Elizabethan age, ensured her transcendence of the world of political praxis. Perhaps Niccols realized this. In his 'Induction,' he thinks 'what a Mirrour she might be / Vnto all future times posteritie' (779); future times, not future officeholders.

Where Baldwin and his collaborators, then, presented an engaged, current, multivocal version of history and historiography that offered a variegated and complex cultural authority of exempla that qualified the authority of bureaucracy, Niccols recreated authority, in

'England's Eliza,' unquestioningly enshrining the prerogatives of
political absolutism in historical panegyric. The immediate past was
stripped of its political import to the present, and a monologic memory
was substituted for a polyvocal history. In the 'Induction,' the ghost of
Elizabeth is given a few words of dialogue. She tells the poet,

> Yet to the world, that I a Mirrour bee
> Amongst those many Mirrours writ by thee;
> Feare neither bite of dogged *Theons* tooth,
> Nor soone-shot bolts of giddie headed youth;
> For th'awfull power of my sole dreaded name,
> Shall from thy verse auert all foule defame   (781)

Her reputation sanctifies the poem, making it invulnerable to criticism,
especially, we might guess, historical criticism. In this last edition of
the *Mirror*, then, the voices of intellectual engagement, of historiography, are to be silenced by the authority of numinous regality.

   While this evolution was in part the product of the declining abilities
of successive authors, it also was linked to those editors' perceptions of
their readership. Whatever the intentions of Baldwin, the *Mirror* had
an avid citizen readership from the beginning.[73] The subsequent editors increasingly attempted to target this lucrative market. So as *A Mirror for Magistrates* moved from polemic to panegyric, as it diverged
from contemporary movements in historiography, it became more and
more a product for the urban reader. Higgins and Blennerhasset, while
purporting to address all estates, constructed cautionary tales of temperance and chastity obviously designed for an urban audience. At the
same time, the narratives became longer, crowded with historical
detail extraneous to the didacticism of the individual historical exemplum. They became pocket histories and/or sentimental tales. Physi-
cally the book changed; Niccols, following the lead of popular works
such as William Jaggard's *A view Of all The Right Honourable the Lord
Mayors of this Honourable Citty of London* (1601), introduced woodcuts
of the tragic subjects. In short, the entertainment value of the *de casibus*
form was highlighted in a bid for wider acceptance.

   But it did not work. At a time when popular literacy and political
consciousness were becoming increasingly dependent, it was mis-
guided of Niccols to offer moral sentiment to a class that read history specifically for its practical political lessons.[74] Early editions of the
Mirror were popular because they were in line with contemporary

historiography and reflected current political concerns; later editions suffered as they evolved away from this authority and agenda towards an outdated perception of urban interests. And so the last edition did not sell; the sheets were reissued three times without success.[75] The addition of 'England's Eliza' to this final edition of the *Mirror* represented Niccols's bid to give the tragic history of England a happy ending, and to mark off the age of political misfortune as past, belonging to the unsettled era before Elizabeth. But by drawing that line between now and then, Niccols finally broke the *Mirror*.

Chapter Three

Tragedy and Fortune

In the previous chapter we looked at *de casibus* literature as a form of history writing and related *A Mirror for Magistrates* to the history traditions of the sixteenth and seventeenth centuries. I began with the question of history in order to break the automatic association of *de casibus* literature with tragedy. I would now like to come back to the question of *de casibus* as tragedy and to examine the relation of the *Mirror* to this literary form.

In general (there is no consistent scholarly practice), literary critics use the term *de casibus* to denote tragedies of fortune – that is, tragedies in which the protagonists fall through no clear fault of their own. Often, however, '*de casibus* tragedy' seems to be the shorthand that Renaissance drama critics use for 'plodding medieval tragedy.' Authors, especially medieval and early Renaissance authors, are applauded or denigrated according to how well they overcome the '*De Casibus* tradition in all its horror.'[1] The unseen measure in this evaluation is Elizabethan dramatic tragedy and the Aristotelian tragic theory.[2] The few thorough explorations of the form, such as those offered by Willard Farnham in *The Medieval Heritage of Elizabethan Tragedy* and Madeleine Doran in *Endeavors of Art*, link the *de casibus* tragedy to the medieval *de contemptu mundi* tradition, then go on to see it as a primitive stage in the evolution towards Shakespeare.[3]

Recognizing a transcendent literary form in Shakespeare's tragedies, then, literary critics have worked backwards to earlier sad stories, classified them as tragedies, and dismissed them as simplistically dependent upon a mechanistic pattern of fortune's retributions, not adequately sophisticated to be considered real tragedy. But having adopted Henry Kelly's solution here in considering as tragedies only those works that their authors deemed tragedies, we must rewrite the history of *de casibus* literature. The progenitor of *de casibus* literature, Boccaccio's *De casibus virorum illustrium*, is not part of the tragic canon. Boccaccio considered his work a history, not a tragedy. But by the time that the *De casibus* became *Fall of Princes*, the idea of tragedy was firmly attached to it and the association has been automatic ever since. What happened?

To find out, let us look at Lydgate's introduction to *Fall of Princes*. Lydgate begins by praising Laurent de Premierfait for translating Boccaccio out of the Latin. He, perhaps self-servingly, notes that 'artificeres' (i.e., translators) have licence to change things 'Fro good to bettir' (1: 20) to 'Make olde thynges for to seeme newe' (1: 28). Lydgate gives a summary of the scope and intention of Boccaccio's original, explaining how the stories please by 'Shewyng a merour how al the world shal faile, / And how Fortune, for al ther hih renoun, / Hath vpon pryncis iuredicccioun' (1: 159–61). He then begins a search for a muse:

> Calliope my callyng will refuse,
> And on Pernaso here worthi sustren alle
> Thei will ther sugre tempre with no galle,
> For ther suetnesse & lusti fressh syngyng
> Full ferr discordith fro materis compleynyng.   (1: 241–5)

Why Lydgate does not consider Melpomene, the muse of tragedy, is unclear. Instead he runs down a list of writers who are associated with tragedy. He begins with 'My maistir Chaucer, with his fresh comedies, / Is ded, allas, cheeff poete off Breteyne, / That whilom made ful pitous tragedies' (1: 242–8), then goes back in time:

> Senek in Rome, thoruh his hih prudence,
> Wrot tragedies of gret moralite;
> And Tullius, cheefe welle of eloquence,
> Maad in his tyme many fressh dite;
> Franceis Petrak, off Florence the cite,
> Made a book, as I can reherce,
> Off too Fortunys, welful and peruerse.   (1: 253–9)

He returns to Boccaccio, who 'wrot maters lamentable, / The fall of pryncies, where he doth expresse / How for ther ioie thei fill in gret distresse' (1: 269–71). Lydgate then circles back to Chaucer, giving a long summary of that poet's output. Finally he concludes

> Dites of murnyng and off compleynynge
> Nat appertene onto Calliope,
> Nor to the Muses, that on Parnaso synge,
> Which be remembrid in noumbre thries thre;
> And onto materes off aduersite,
> With ther sugred aureat licour
> Thei be nat willi for to doon fauour;
>
> But off disdeyn me settyng ferr a-bak
> To hyndre me off that I wolde endite,
> Hauyng no colous but onli whit & blak,
> To the tragedies which that I shal write.
> And for I can my-silff no bet acquite,
> Vndir support off all that shal it reede,
> Vpon Bochas riht thus I will proceede.   (1: 456–9)

Boccaccio will be Lydgate's muse, but Chaucer, Seneca, Tullius, and Petrarch are his tragedians.[4] The *De casibus virorum illustrium* may be the Lydgate's source material, but Lydgate did not consider it primarily a tragedy. While he refers to individual stories that he treats from Boccaccio as tragedies, he avoids the term in his introductory remarks on Boccaccio and his work.

This omission may occur because Lydgate, like Boccaccio and most of his contemporaries, believed tragedy to be an extinct performative art. Lydgate envisions a tragic performance in his *Troy Book*:

> And whilom thus was halwed the memorie
> Of tragedies, as bokis make mynde,
> Whan thei wer rad or songyn, as I fynde,
> In the theatre ther was a smal auter
> Amyddes set, that was half circuler,
> Whiche in-to the Est of custom was directe;
> Vp-on the whiche a pulpet was erecte,
> And ther-in stod a aw[n]cien poete,
> For to reherse by rethorikes swete
> Th noble dedis, that were historial,
> Of kynges, princes for a memorial   (2: 860–70)[5]

While the poet was 'singinge his dites' of historical lives,

> There cam out men gastful of her cheris,
> Disfigurid her casis with viseris,
> Pleying by signes in the peples siyt,
> That the poete songon hath on hiyt   (2: 901–4)

The point of the poet's songs was to demonstrate

> How pitously thei made her mortal ende
> Thoruy fals Fortune, that al the world wil schende,
> And how the fyn of al her worthines
> Endid in sorwe and [in] hiye tristesse   (2: 883–6)

Lydgate, then, imagined a performance sung by a poet and illustrated by masked dancers or mimes. The songs told the lives of historical great personages who, trusting 'fals Fortune,' met sad ends.

The notion that *de casibus* is also tragedy came from Chaucer, the second most discussed author after Boccaccio in Lydgate's introduction. Lydgate praises Chaucer for *Troilus and Cresyde* and translating Boethius (1: 281–92). He recites a catalogue of Chaucer's works. And he commends *The Canterbury Tales*, mentioning three of the tales in particular:

> In prose he wrot the Tale off Melibe,
> And off his wiff, that callid was Prudence,
> And off Grisildis parfit pacience,
> And how the Monk off stories newe & olde
> Pitous tragedies be the weie tolde.   (1: 346–50)

It is *The Monk's Tale* that is of interest here, for it was the first English *de casibus*, influential as one of Chaucer's best-loved tales in the fifteenth century.[6] More important, it marks the point at which, in the English tradition at least, *de casibus* shifted from a being a vision of history to also being a form of tragic literature.

The Monk's Tale's title alone marks it as significant for this study: '*Heere bigynneth the Monkes Tale De Casibus Virorum Illustrium.*' Chaucer was consciously working in the tradition set by Boccaccio. The tale follows Boccaccio's original in being a collection of short tales of the falls of great personages, arranged in rough chronological order, beginning with Lucifer and ending, when cut off by the Knight, with Croesus,

King of Lydia. Indeed, it has been suggested that *The Monk's Tale* represents an insertion, by Chaucer, of an earlier independent work, one based very closely on Boccaccio's *De casibus* and probably written just after Chaucer had returned from his first trip to Italy (1372–3). This goes some way towards explaining the inconsistencies in the tale and its prologue (e.g., the unfulfilled promise of a life of Saint Edward) and some of the manuscript problems associated with the text.[7] Chaucer's sources for the tales in *The Monk's Tale* included the Vulgate, *Roman de la Rose, Metamorphosis, Heriodes, De claris mulieribus*, the *Inferno*, and, of course, *De casibus* itself. His version of the Samson story comes almost directly from Boccaccio's original.[8]

Indeed, Chaucer was acquainted enough with the *de casibus* form to parody it in other parts of *The Canterbury Tales*. Immediately after *The Monk's Tale* comes *The Nun's Priest's Tale* of Chauntecleer and Pertelote, the cock and hen. Chauntecleer recites a *de casibus*–style list of histories, of which each proves that dreams predict the truth. The Pardoner, in his tale, gives a short list of great men felled by gluttony.

But *The Monk's Tale* does more than just repeat in miniature Boccaccio's literary form. It introduces the idea of tragedy to the *de casibus* form. In fact, the tale gives not one, but two definitions of tragedy. The first comes in the tale's prologue. The Monk tells his fellow travellers,

> Or ellis, first, tragedies wol I telle,
> Of whiche I have an hundred in my celle.
> Tragedie is to seyn a certeyn storie,
> As olde bookes maken us memorie,
> Of hym that stood in greet prosperitee,
> And is yfallen out of heigh degree
> Into myserie, and endeth wrecchedly.
> And they ben versified communely
> Of six feet, which men clepen *exametron*.
> In prose eek been endited many oon,
> And eek in meetre, in many a sondry wyse.   (VII: 1971–81)[9]

This is the only detailed description of a literary genre offered by a pilgrim in *The Canterbury Tales*.

The tale itself begins with another definition of tragedy:

> I wol biwaille in manere of tragedie
> The harm of hem that stoode in heigh degree,

And fillen so that ther nas no remedie
To brynge hem out of hir adversitee.   (VII: 1991–4)

And speculation on the didactic import of the form:

For certein, whan that Fortune list to flee,
Ther may no man the cours of hire withholde.
Lat no man truste on blynd prosperitee;
Be war by thise ensamples trewe and olde.   (VII: 1995–8)

The final insistence on the veracity and antiquity of the about-to-
be preferred examples takes us back into the realm of history, but
what is of interest here is the definition of tragedy. Where did it come
from?

D.W. Robertson, Jr offered an answer years ago: 'Chaucer found the
definition of tragedy which he followed in the Monk's Tale imbedded
in a discussion of fortune in the De consolatione.'[10] The lines come in
Book 2, Prosa 2, of Boece, Chaucer's translation of the Boethius's De consolatione philosophiae. The figure of Philosophy, to cure Boethius of the
belief that he has been betrayed by fortune, takes on Fortune's voice
and offers a first-person rationalization of her behaviour. She gives
examples of extreme swings in fortune: the lives of Croesus of Lydia
(the last story recited in The Monk's Tale) and Aemilius Paulus. Then she
asks, 'What other thynge bywaylen the cryinges of tragedyes but oonly
the dedes of Fortune, that with an unwar strook overturneth the
realmes of greet nobleye?' (ii. pr. 2, 67–70). A couple of ideas emerge
from this rhetorical question: tragedy is the literary record of the vagaries of fortune; tragedy is class specific. But, as Monica E. McAlpine
points out, 'Boethius' purpose here ... is not to define a literary genre
but to call emphatic attention, by means of a rhetorical question, to the
thematic contents of some classical tragedies. The rhetorical question is
followed by allusions to two such tragedies, and the questions and the
allusions together constitute merely an ornament of the larger argument.'[11] Chaucer offers a parenthetical definition of tragedy after the
Boethian allusion to the form: 'Glose. Tragedye is to seyn a dite of a prosperite for a tyme, that endeth in wrecchidnesse' (ii. pr. 2, 70–2). This gloss is a
translation of the Latin definition provided by the Oxford professor
Nicolas Trevet in the copy-text of Boethius that Chaucer used. Chaucer
made one significant change to Trevet's definition, eliminating the professor's requirement that tragedy must deal with vicious or criminal
protagonists.[12] For Chaucer, 'wrecchidnesse' could befall anyone.

Chaucer critics have jumped on this gloss and tried to relate it to *The Monk's Tale*, primarily through an exploration of the question of fortune. D.W. Robertson, Jr's comment is typical: 'It is fairly obvious that Chaucer's conception of tragedy is dependent on his conception of Fortune, and that we cannot understand what he meant by *tragedy* unless we understand also what he meant by *Fortune*, and what happens "whan men trusteth hire."'[13] In fact, the critical fixation on fortune is simply not in line with definitions of tragedy that Chaucer offers. Clearly it is not in his glossed definition in the *Boece*. It is not part of the first definition, the one offered in the prologue, of *The Monk's Tale*. Nor is it an intrinsic part of the second definition, the one that begins the tale. It comes *after* that definition, a signpost to the didactic potential of the form, but not a definition of the form itself. Robertson's comment is indicative of the fact that, to a large degree, Chaucer critics' readings of the tragedy definitions are skewed by their critical applications. The majority of them do not use the definitions, except in passing, to examine *The Monk's Tale* at all; instead, they use them as a jumping-off point to leap to what they really want to discuss, *Troilus and Criseyde*, a work in which the role of fortune, and the cryptic reference to 'litel myn tragedye' (V· 1786), seem central.

In *The Monk's Tale*, fortune is simply not that important. *The Monk's Tale* begins with very short (eight lines each) renditions of the falls of Lucifer and Adam. Neither of these falls involves fortune. Chaucer makes this point specifically in the Lucifer story – 'For though Fortune may noon angel dere, / From heigh degree yet fel he for his synne / Down into helle' (VII: 2001–3) – and implies it in the Adam story: 'Hadde nevere worldly man so heigh degree / As Adam, til he for mysgovernaunce / Was dryven out of hys hye prosperitee / To labour' (VII: 2011–14). So Chaucer begins his *de casibus* with the two most famous and significant falls in the Christian tradition, both of which are dependent upon free will rather than capricious fortune. The next tragedy, a much longer one, is of Samson. Again, fortune plays no part. Edward M. Socola has argued that 'in Chaucer's mind the three biblical characters dealt directly with God, without Fortune as an intermediary, for nowhere in his writings does Chaucer link the names of Lucifer, Adam, or Samson with Fortune.'[14] Possibly, or else fortune is simply not as central to Chaucer's vision of tragedy as the critics have assumed. Fortune does not appear in the tragedy of Nebuchadnezzar nor in the short tragedy of Barnabò Visconti, and critics have had to launch ingenious readings of the stories to account for this absence.[15]

Annoyingly, Chaucer's Monk does not even offer tales that consistently illustrate the cause–effect relation between evil actions and personal destruction. The protagonists of 'De Petro Rege de Cipro' and 'De Barnabo de Lumbardia' are both good men betrayed. De Petro is killed 'for no thyng but for thy chivalrie' (VII: 2395) and Barnabò's death offers no moral at all: 'But why ne how noot I that thou were slawe' (VII: 2406). Alexander the Great is depicted as the greatest of men, betrayed and poisoned by followers. His story serves to 'endite / False Fortune, and poyson to despise' (VII: 2668–9) but offers no relation between moral failing and decline. Julius Caesar, too, in the Monk's telling, is a great man who rose 'By wisedom, manhede, and by greet labour, / From humble bed to roial magestee' (VII: 2670–1) only to be assassinated by 'false Brutus' that 'ever hadde of his hye estaat envye' (VII: 2698).

Critics have attempted to explain these apparent contradictions – the absence of fortune from some tales, the death of good men – as part of *The Monk's Tale*'s drama. William C. Strange argues that the Monk offers a series of tales that he knows are contradictory and, befuddled by this awareness, attempts to oscillate between different types of stories. 'Then, the movement back and forth becomes faster and faster until the two extremes collapse into a single, grinding climax with Croesus.'[16] Jahan Ramazani has argued a psychology of the Monk based on his fastidious definition and its careful fulfilment in the tales he tells; he has psychoanalysed the Monk to reveal the 'anal psychology of collection and suppressed aggression that underlies his rhetoric.'[17] Joella Owens Brown argues that *The Monk's Tale* is supposed to be dull and contradictory; Chaucer is parodying an 'accurately documented, well-constructed sermon, albeit a dull one.'[18]

All of these readings are overly ingenious. To accuse *The Monk's Tale* of being dull, and the Monk of being anal for collecting stories, is simply not to understand the *de casibus* form or the exemplary mode. It makes its teleological point through repetition. To offer elaborate schemes to rationalize the apparent contradictions in the tragic form, regarding fortune or the culpability of the tragic victims, is to miss another point: history is not consistent. Boccaccio's tales are not consistent in these regards. Why should they be? The simpler answer to the apparent contradictions in the tale is that fortune is not the determining factor in Chaucer's conception of tragedy.

But Chaucer is vitally important to the development of the *de casibus* form for two reasons. First, it was Chaucer who took Boccaccio's historical model and saw in it the classical tragic narrative arc: '*Tragedye is to seyn a dite of a prosperite for a tyme, that endeth in wrecchidnesse.*' Boccaccio did not identify the *metabasis*-dominated biography as tragic, but Chaucer did. Chaucer arrived at this insight by defining tragedy by its story line, not by the import of that story line, which was Boccaccio's primary concern. While the story that 'endeth in wrecchidnesse' *may* be used to teach us lessons about the instability of Dame Fortune, it does not have to; this was why Chaucer adds the idea of fortune *after* his second definition of the form in *The Monk's Tale*. As long as the story ends unhappily, it is a tragedy.

The second of Chaucer's insights was that tragedy is supposed to evoke empathy in the reader. The Monk promises that he will '*biwaille in manere of tragedie / The harm of hem that stoode in heigh degree.*' Bewail in Chaucer means to express great sorrow for, to lament loudly, to mourn. It is a word he used in both *Troilus* and *Boece*. What is being bewailed in *The Monk's Tale* is the terrible fates of those who fall. Boccaccio did not bewail his characters, though he lamented the repercussions of their falls. The stories of Boccaccio's characters are held up for inspection rather than sympathy. As he said in his introduction, 'from among the mighty I shall select the most famous, so when our princes see these rulers, old and spent, prostrated by the judgment of God, they will recognize God's power, the shiftiness of Fortune, and their own insecurity. They will learn the bounds of their merry-making, and by the misfortunes of others, they can take counsel for their own profit' (2). Boccaccio was here perfectly in line with other writers of non-fiction in the Middle Ages and early Renaissance.

> There were recognized literary genres in the Middle Ages dealing with disaster and death, notably lives of famous men, lives of saints, cautionary exempla, and complaints. But the first three of these genres concentrated on praising or blaming the victims or perpetrators, while the fourth normally stressed the author's own loss and eliminated any story element. There was no generic demand for the sort of empathetic sorrow for the disasters of others that both Aristotle and Chaucer required of tragedy.[19]

It is no wonder that Lydgate praised *The Monk's Tale* for its relation of '*pitous* tragedies'; pity is just what the *de casibus* form needed to make it more than history. Again, it is significant that, in the introduction to *Fall of Princes*, Lydgate did not use the word 'tragedy' in conjunction with Boccaccio, the original author of the 'stories' he had translated. It is only when Lydgate turns his attention to Chaucer that the word 'tragedy' is introduced: 'cheeff poete off Breteyne, / That whilom made ful pitous tragedies' (1: 247–8). Lydgate understood, as so many recent Chaucer critics have not, the importance of Chaucer to the *de casibus* tradition.

Lydgate himself, in *Fall of Princes*, oscillated between Boccaccio's moral history and Chaucer's 'pitous' tragedies. In the spirit of Boccaccio, he delivered injunctions, usually in his envoys:

> Noble Pryncis, heer ye may weel see
> As in a merour, off ful cleer euydence,
> Be many exaumple mo than too or three,
> What harm folweth off slouth & necligence   (2: 2528–31)

The address to rulers here, the invocation of the mirror as a symbol of introspection, and the insistence on the number of stories are all marks of *de casibus* history. But, unlike Boccaccio, Lydgate often calls his stories 'tragedies' and, in Chaucerian fashion, 'biwailles' the fate of the tales' protagonists. The story of Priam, for example, is a 'tragedie pitous & lamentable / And dolerous to writen & expresse' (1: 6308–9).

In the prologue to Book II, Lydgate explicitly tried to reconcile history and tragedy:

> To summe folk, parcas, it wolde seeme,
> Touchyng the chaunges & mutabilities
> Bi me rehersid, that thei myhte deeme,
> Off Fortunes straunge aduersites
> To pryncis shewed, doun pullid from ther sees,
> The tragedies auhte inouh suffise
> In compleynyng, which ye han herd deuise.   (2: 1–7)

But in the *de casibus* history tradition, enough never suffices. Lydgate was worried about his reader, not because there was a danger of overstating his historical point, but because of the emotional impact of the narrative form:

> The stori pitous, the processe lamentable,
> Void off ioie, al gladnesse and plesaunce,

A thyng to greuous and to inportable,
Where-as no merthe is medlid with greuanunce,
Al upon compleynt standith thalliaunce,
Most whan Fortune, who that hir cours weel knewe,
Chaungith old ioie into sorwes newe.   (2: 8–14)

Lydgate seemed to be anticipating Chaucer's Knight's objection to *The Monk's Tale*:

namoore of this!
That ye han seyd is right ynough, ywis,
And muchel moore; for litel hevynesse
Is right ynough to muche folk, I gesse.   (VII: 2767–70)

But Lydgate persisted in these stories of 'such vnwar chaung, such vnkouth wrechidnesse' (2: 19) because 'The fall off on is a cleer lanterne / To teche a-nother what he shal eschewe' (2: 29–30).

Lydgate then goes on to attack the vexed issue of fortune in tragic stories. Here he is governed by his political concerns, and he denies an arbitrary fortune: 'It is nat she that pryncis gaff the fall, / But vicious lyuyng, pleynli to endite' (2: 45–6). Indeed, 'Fortune hath no domynacioun, / Wher noble pryncis be gouerned be resoun' (2: 55–6). That is the theory, anyway. In practice, it is hard to find stories in Lydgate's version that fit this reassuringly mechanical equation. For example, when Lydgate comes to the story of Priam of Troy, he explains that he does not have to copy out the story because he dealt with it earlier in his *Troy Book*. That book was written at the request of Henry V, 'most myhti off puissance' (1: 5959), defender of the church, bringer of peace. 'But, o allas, ageyn deth is no boone! This lond may seyn he deied al to soone' (1: 5977–8).

Cavendish, in *Metrical Visions*, followed the lead of Lydgate in the questions of both tragedy and fortune. In the prologue of the book, tragedy is not clearly distinquished from history. Indeed, the narrator implies that his tragic stories should be judged, and corrected, as history:

Thoughe I onworthe / this tragedy do begyne
Of pardon I pray / the reders in meke wyse
And to correct / where they se fault therin.
Reputyng it for lake / of connyng exercyse.   (50–3)

Fortune is invoked by most of the ghosts who step forward to complain, but often the invocation is at odds with a simultaneous admission of moral culpability and acknowledgment of God's justice. So Anne Boleyn's brother, Viscount Rochford, has it both ways:

> Ffor where God lyst to punyshe / a man of Right
> By mortall sword / farewell all resistence.
> Whan grace fayllyth / honor hathe no force or myght
> Of nobilitie also / it defacyth the highe preemynence
> And chayngythe ther power / to feoble impotence /
> Than tornyth ffortune / hir whele most spedely.
> Example tak of me / for my lewde avoultrie   (323–9)

While confessing his lechery – the historical Rochford was executed for purportedly conducting an incestuous relationship with his sister, the Queen – he enjoins readers to remember 'that all standythe on ffortune' (336). Cavendish makes no sustained attempt to explain the relation of fortune to providence or moral failing.

What, then, are we to make of the issue of fortune in the *de casibus* tradition before *A Mirror for Magistrates*? Part of the confusion is cultural rather than literary. Though one of the most prevalent images of the Middle Ages and Renaissance, fortune embodies a concept that has no place in a divinely ordered, providential universe. On the other hand, 'Fortune was regarded in the Middle Ages as a useful designation for an idea which fitted nicely into the scheme of Christian theology. One did not "believe in" Fortune any more than one believed in the goddess Venus; but Fortune, like Venus, was used to express a kind of behaviour to which almost everyone is subject.'[20] The one reference to Fortune in the Bible was helpful here:

> But you who forsake the LORD,
>   who forget my holy mountain,
> who set a table for Fortune
>   and fill cups of mixed wine for Destiny;
> I will destine you to the sword,
>   and all of you shall bow down to the slaughter.   (Isa. 65: 11–12)

Christian thinkers, loath to lose the rich iconography of the goddess, represented her in a number of ways. Dante, for example, enlisted her into the hierarchy of avenging angels. Others conflated the goddess with other classical emblems, such as Nemesis, that were more easily reconciled with a Christian universe.[21] Historians such Edward Hall used her as a synonym for divine justice, a convenient personification of the acts of providence.[22]

Boccaccio presented what is tantamount to a Christian denial of sublunar providence. In his vision of history, God seems to have turned the world over to fortune, making *metabasis* all but inevitable and wholly arbitrary. The philosophical reaction to this vision is *contemptus mundi*; because the world is inconstant and unjust, one should focus all attention on the next, where fortune has no play. The teleology of world history was assumed to be the product of an irrational sublunary force, fortune, that stands in opposition to the rational eternity of the next world. Boccaccio employed this vision of history for satiric ends, launching into scathing attacks on worldly vain princes. Fortune 'enables him to stress the interdependence between monarchical authority and the historical realm in which it operates.'[23]

Chaucer's concern was as much with tragedy, that is, piteous stories that end in wretchedness, as with history. The Monk even apologizes in the tale's prologue for not being stricter about the historical arrangement of his material: 'But first I yow biseeke in this mateere, / Though I by ordre tell nat thise thynges' (VII: 1984–5). Caught between tragedy and history, *The Monk's Tale* invokes or fails to invoke fortune or moral culpability, depending on the story at hand. Lydgate's response was appropriately more monkish and measured: he advocated a course of moral asceticism to avoid being carried aloft and down on Fortune's wheel. He argued that fortune applied only to the wicked, though the historical record would seem to confute this reassuring formula. He attempted a compromise between Boccaccio's historical vision and Chaucer's tragic empathy; the result is closer to Boccaccio. Cavendish used the idea of fortune indiscriminately.

As discussed in the previous chapter, the authors of the early editions of *A Mirror for Magistrates* were thinking in terms of history, not tragedy, when they sat down to compile their books. The first person mentioned in the work is Plato, not Aristotle. The word 'tragedy' does not appear in Baldwin's dedication to the first edition of the book. Indeed, the preface to the first tragedy sets a tone of Boccaccio-like censure: 'I wyll take vpon me the miserable person of syr Robert Tresilian chiefe Iustice of Englande, and of other which suffred with him: thereby to warne all of his authorytie and profession, to take heed of wrong

Iudgementes, mysconstruyng of lawes, or wrestyng the same to serue the princes turnes, whiche ryghtfullye brought theym to a myserable ende, which they may iustly lament in maner ensuyng' (1: 71). And the ghost of Tresilian himself begins his story with a finger-wagging injunction: 'Learne by vs ye Lawyers and Iudges of the lande / Vncorrupt and vpryght in doome alway to stande' (1: 73). The misery that the story recounts is not presented to elicit empathy from the reader, then, but rather to frighten the powerful into virtue.

But the envoy that follows the tale begins 'whan maister *Ferrers* had finished this tragedye, whiche semed not vnfyt for the persons touched in the same' (1: 81). This is the first time the word 'tragedy' appears in the *Mirror*. The same envoy continues to discuss the upcoming story, the tale of the two Mortimers, 'whose historye syth it is notable and the example fruitfull' (1: 81). A similar oscillation between the terms 'tragedy' and 'history' occurs in the envoy comment after the Mortimers' story: 'After that this Tragedy was ended, mayster *Ferrers* sayde: seyng it is best to place eche person in his ordre, *Baldwin* take you the Chronicles and marke them as they cum' (1: 91). The stories are tragedies, but they are to be treated with the precision of histories. This juggling between tragedy and history goes on throughout the prose envoys of the Baldwin editions of the *Mirror*. At times empathy for the protagonists will be foregrounded: 'Whan he had ended this so wofull a tragedy, and to all Princes a ryght wurthy instruction, we paused: hauing passed through a miserable time full of piteous tragedyes' (1: 119). Sometimes this empathy will even transcend the obvious political didacticism of the biography at hand. So, in the story of King James I of Scotland, we are told that he is a 'tragicall person in deede' (1: 154), but the title of the tale declares 'how king Iames the first for breaking his othes and bondes, was by gods suffrauns miserably murdred of his owne subiects' (1: 155). A pitiable end, yes, but a politically justified one.

The most obviously 'pitous' poem of the early editions of the *Mirror* is Sackville's 'Induction,' which appeared in the second Baldwin edition of 1563. The envoy before the 'Induction' is concerned with history. In that envoy, the inclusion of the 'Induction' is justified by Sackville's plan to take all of the *Mirror* tragedies written so far, put them in one volume, 'and from that time backeward euen to the time of William the conquerour ... to continue and perfect all the story ... in such order as Lydgate (folowing Bocchas) had already vsed' (1: 297). In other words, Sackville envisioned the *Mirror* that would eventually be written: a comprehensive *de casibus* history of England. The 'Induction' was to be the introduction to this comprehensive history, but Sackville never wrote the promised history.

The 'Induction' traces the adventures of a narrator who, lamenting the 'wrathful winter prochinge on a pace' (1: 298), wanders about in a landscape of such overwhelming pathetic fallacy that the stellar constellations themselves seem to warn of impending misery.[24] This environment teaches the narrator that 'all earthly thinges be borne / To dye the death, for nought long time may last. / The sommers beauty yeeldes to winters blast' (1: 300). This leads him to a conveniently self-referential notion:

> My busie minde presented vnto me
> Such fall of pieres as in this realme had be:
> That ofte I wisht some would their woes descryue.
> To warne the rest whom fortune left aliue.   (1: 300)

Immediately the narrator encounters a 'piteous wight' who takes him to the underworld. On the way they encounter the allegorical figures of Remorse, Dread, Revenge, Misery, Care, Sleep, Old Age, Malady, Famine, Death, and War before being ferried across Lake Acheron by 'grisly Charon' to Pluto's realm, where 'Prynces of renowne, / That whilom sat on top of Fortunes wheele / Nowe layed ful lowe, like wretches whurled downe' (1: 316). There they meet Henry, Duke of Buckingham, who recounts his tragedy. The entire sequence, up to the moment the that Henry steps forward, comes almost directly from the *Aeneid*.[25] Sackville took the list of allegorical characters loitering around the gates of hell from Vergil and expanded the descriptions of each character, but he did not merely decorate Vergil; he diverged from Vergil in one very crucial matter. Whereas, in the *Aeneid*, Aeneas was led on his trip to the underworld by the Sibyl, in Sackville's 'Induction' the poet is led by the character of Sorrow. This character, who may owe something to the character of Sorrow in Chaucer's translation of *The Romaunt of the Rose*, sets the tone for the 'Induction' and the tragedy that follow.[26] She explains that she has just left the realm of Pluto:

> Whence come I am, the drery destinie
> And luckles lot for to bemone of those,
> Whom Fortune in this maze of miserie

Of wretched chaunce most wofull myrrours chose
That when thou seest how lightly they did lose
Theyr pompe, theyr power, & that they thought most sure,
Thou mayest soone deeme no earthly ioye may dure.   (1: 302)

The pathetic fallacy of the 'Induction,' the guide Sorrow, and the
allegorical figures combine to make Sackville's 'Induction' less politically pointed than other sections of the Baldwin editions of the *Mirror*.
The 'Induction' seeks to invoke melancholy and empathy, not censure.
For example, when the narrator sees the last of the allegorical figures
outside of hell, War, he is spurred to remember great battles and war-
riors of antiquity. This short list culminates in the remembrance of
Troy. The vision of a fallen Troy has a political import: 'by her fall we
learne, / That cities, towres, wealth, world, and al shall quayle' (1:
313). But, most of all, it invokes sorrow. Sackville takes six stanzas to,
in the best Chaucerian tradition, bewail: 'O Troy, Troy, there is no
boote but bale' (1: 314). Sackville swings the *Mirror* in the direction of
tragedy, placing more emphasis on the fear and pity of the narrative of
decline than on its historical/political implications. The tragedy that
follows the 'Induction,' 'Henry, Duke of Buckingham,' also emphasizes pity. Buckingham, henchman of Richard III, is given to falling
into fits during the recounting of his life: 'And groveling flat vpon the
ground he lay, / Which with his teeth he al to gnasht and gnawed' (1:
343). The effect is melodramatic but, interestingly, does not seem to
move Baldwin and his friends: in the envoy that follows, the editors
are more concerned with whether Sackville has invoked the papist
concept of purgatory in this description of the underworld than they
are in the sorrowful plight of Buckingham.

Indeed, the next tragedy, 'The Poet Collingbourne,' seems an antidote to the maudlin pity of the Sackville section. Collingbourne, executed by Richard III for a treasonous rhyme ('The Cat, the Rat, and
Lovel our Dog, / Do rule all England under a Hog'), exhorts Baldwin
to 'Withdrawe thy pen, for nothing shalt thou gayne / Save hate, with
losse of paper, ynke and payne' (1: 349). The perfect poet must be
'nymble, free, and swyft' and protected by the 'Poetes auncient liber-
ties' (1: 354). The political import of this tragedy is obvious. Collingbourne is presented as a martyr of free poetic expression, the political
poet who, hindsight tells us, was astute in his assessment of the political tenor of his times. He is the prototype of Baldwin and his collective.
Indeed, Collingbourne specifically addresses Baldwin's project:

Thy entent I knowe is godly, playne, and good,
To warne the wyse, to fraye the fond fro yll:
But wycked worldelinges are so wytles wood,
That to the wurst they all thinges construe styl.   (1: 349)

There is nothing here about empathy for the fallen. The project is political, not emotional.

The remainder of the Baldwin editions tend towards the Collingbourne model; they emphasize the political and historical over the
tragic and the empathetic. The tragedy of Shore's Wife, which is discussed in the next chapter, is the most notable exception to this rule.

Higgins, in the introduction to the *First Part of the Mirror for Magistrates*, repeatedly makes use of the term 'tragedy' to describe the biographies in his book. He, as we have seen in the previous chapter, is
adamant in claiming that he is writing history, but he tells us every one
of the personages he is about to describe 'playde his tragoedye' (2: 43).
After his prose introduction, Higgins begins his addition to the *Mirror*
with an author's induction that is clearly modelled on Sackville's
'Induction.' It starts with some heavy-handed pathetic fallacy, then
leads to the narrator finding a 'booke so sad,' the *Mirror*:

A Mirroure well it may be calde a glasse,
More cleare then any crystall vnder Sun,
In eache respecte, the Tragoedies so passe,
Their names shall lyue, that such a worke begun   (2: 41)

The rest of Higgins's induction is not especially empathetic, and the
first biography of his *Mirror*, while invoking tragedy ('My life and
death, a Tragedye so true' says Albanact, son of Brutus), is a sweeping
recounting of Britain's mythological founding by Brutus that ends
when Albanact is killed, almost arbitrarily, in a battle with invading
Huns. The only lesson that the story teaches the ghost of Albanact,
beside not trusting fortune, is the 'rashness was the cause of all my
woe' (2: 69). The rest of the stories in Higgins's *Mirror* follow a similar
pattern: after a few platitudes about fortune, the history of the life is
repeated until death comes, often very suddenly. After death, the
ghost may have a stanza or two to warn the readers not to follow his
example and to avoid wickedness.

Perhaps the closest that Higgins comes to generating pity for the victims of tragedy is in the three stories of women: Elstride, the concubine

of Locrinus; Sabrine, her daughter; and Cordila. The first two were drowned by the Locrinus's jealous wife, Gwendoline. We will examine how these stories fit into the representation of women in the *Mirror* tradition in the next chapter, but here let us note that Higgins lays on the pathos with a trowel. When Estride and Sabrine are confronted by Gwendoline, Sabrine throws herself on the ground and begs that she should die rather than her mother: 'Which when I sawe the kindnes of the childe, / It burst my harte much more then dome of death' (2: 97). The plea does not work; Elstride bids farewell to the world – 'Adew my pleasures paste, farewell, adew' – and her brave child, then is drowned. If this were not enough, the story of Sabrine recounts the same tale from the child's point of view. The tragedy of Cordila is similarly sentimental. Her story spends an inordinate amount of space recounting the horrors of imprisonment: 'From palace proude, in prison poore to lye: / From kingdomes twayne, to dungion one no more / From Ladies in wayting, vnto vermine store' (2: 155). In this state, Cordila is visited by Despair, who leads her to suicide.

Of the last two editors of the *Mirror*, little can be said about their notions of tragedy, because they use the word indiscriminately. The term seems, by the time the book reached them, to have been watered down to the point where it was no longer denotative; as it had for Cavendish, it had become a literary handle to be grasped, but not a narrative concept to be understood. Thomas Blennerhasset, in the introductory letter attached to *The Second Part of the Mirror for Magistrates*, uses the word 'tragedy' to describe the type of stories he is writing, though he often mixes it with the term 'history' – 'Carassus hauing finished his Tragicall History' (2: 410) – or implies an alignment of history and tragedy: 'Geue leaue therefore good *Memory*, I may / Not here repeate my tedious Tragedy' (2: 425) says the ghost of Vortiger. And, while Blennerhasset spends more time on the emotional profiles of his ghosts than does Higgins, there is no attempt to generate increased sympathy for their plights from this emphasis.

Niccols, in the induction to *A Winter Nights Vision*, says his muse 'must now record the tragicke deeds of great Heroes dead' (555). The induction – now a formal part of the *Mirror* tradition – has the narrator wandering, once more, through a wintery landscape of pathetic fallacy, then retiring to fall asleep while reading a copy of the *Mirror*:

There did I see triumphant death beneath his feet tread downe
The state of Kings, the purple robe, the scepter and the crowne;

Without respect with deadly dart all Princes he did strike,
The vertuous and the vicious Prince to him been both alike   (557)

And Fame shall summon up the ghosts of all those worthie men,
That mongst our Mirrours are not found, that each one orderly
May come to thee, to tell the truth of his sad tragedie.   (560)

The first tragedy in Niccols's book is that of King Arthur. Arthur's ghost admonishes Niccols: 'thou pen-man of Mnemosynie, / Giue heedfull eare vnto my tragedie' (562). And the word 'tragedy' or 'tragic' is applied to almost every biography in *A Winter Nights Vision*. Indeed, the obviously sentimental story of 'The two yong Princes' is followed by 'The Tragicall Life and Death of King Richard the third' (749). Even archvillains can lead tragic lives.

The question of the relation among empathy, history, and tragedy is, as we have seen, bound up in the issues of providence and fortune. If the *de casibus* form demonstrates, as Lydgate claimed his version would, that only the evil are punished and such punishment is inescapable, then the possibility for empathy is slight. The form becomes, as it is for Boccaccio, a satirical *memento mori*. If, however, tragic *metabasis* effects the bad, the good, and the indifferent, then empathy for the plights of some is natural. The possibility for a consistent, and therefore instructive, political teleology, however, is lost and the vagaries of history must be put down to capricious fortune.

As we have seen, the *Mirror* is rigid in asserting a force of schematic retribution, and hence providence, at work in *this* world. And yet even those sinners that it depicts as receiving such obviously deserved ends as being devoured by wolves are given to invoking or cursing fortune. This dichotomy of purpose gives way to chaos in such tragedies as that of William, Duke of Suffolk. The prose introduction to that tale explains that the tragedy will describe 'one of the chiefest of duke Humfreyes destroyers, who by the prouidens of God, came shortly after in such hatred of the people, that the King him selfe could not saue hym from a straunge and notable death' (1: 161). The title notes that he 'was worthily punyshed for abusing his Kyng and causing the destruction of good Duke Humfrey' (1: 162). Yet, Duke William himself declares: 'My only life in all poyntes may suffise / To shewe how base all baytes of Fortune be' (1: 162). The unhappy ghost seems to be moving towards a Lydgatian detente with 'Good hap with vices can not long agree, / Which bring best fortunes to the basest fall' (1: 162), but this is not consistent with 'Wherby I note that Fortune can not raise, / Any one aloft without sum others wracke' (1: 163). We are led to wonder: Why not? The poem ends with an injunction to moral uprightness that obviously assumes the retributive force of providence, yet the editors' final comment in the tale is highly ambiguous:

> Every man reioyced to heare of a wicked man so maruaylously well punished: For though Fortune in many poyntes be iniurius to Princes, yet in this and such lyke she is moost righteous: And only deserveth the name of a Goddes, whan she prouideth meanes to punish & distroye Tyrantes ... It is wurth the labour ... to way the workes and iudgementes of God. (1: 170)

When not engaged in such occultation, the authors of the Baldwin editions make furtive attempts at a reconciliation of fortune and providence:

> Now if this happe wherby we yelde our mynde
> To lust and wyll, be fortune, as we name her,
> Than is she iuftly called false and blynde,
> And no reproche can be to much blame her:
> Yet is the shame our owne when so we shame her,
> For sure this hap if it be rightly knowen,
> Cummeth of our selves, and so the blame our owne.   (Jack Cade, 1: 172)

'Fortune,' in this formulation, is synonymous with the moral defects in ourselves that must inevitably lead to unhappiness. This is taken further in the tragedy of Lord Hastings:

> A heathen god they hold, whoe fortune keepe,
> To deal them happs, whyle god they ween a sleepe.
> Mocke godds they are, and many Gods induce,
> Whoe fortune fayne to father theyr abuse.   (1: 288)

It is a form of paganism to invoke fortune as the cause of our miseries, for this denies the agency of providence.

The last two examples are exceptions to the rule that the *Mirror* exchanges terms of providence and fortune with utter abandon. Even when the text is manifestly exhibiting its dependence upon the Christian concept of history and a rigid scheme of retribution, as it is in the later editions, the content is rife with references to an antithetical set of principles coalesced in the figure of fortune. This tendency has caused much critical confusion, but it should not.[27] The Renaissance mind had a vast capacity for holding logical oppositions in tandem.

In fact, this apparent opposition does not create literary, or even historical, chaos. *A Mirror for Magistrates* isolates and elucidates that part of English history running from the reign of Brute to the reign of Elizabeth. This is both a segment and a microcosm of the totality of Christian history. At any point could be drawn a vertical axis to represent the scale of nature. This would be a cross-section of the hierarchical relationships between all things at that instant. These are two ways of perceiving reality: the horizontal is the diachronic, the study of phenomena within their chronological framework; the vertical is the synchronic, the study of the interrelationships of phenomena in a given instant, without reference to historical context.

In *de casibus* tragedy, the perception of reality is diachronic: the uniqueness of events is emphasized so as to bring out the broad providential pattern they form within the finite confines of time. The ticking of the clock ensures an inexorable pressure towards the Last Judgment, and, in the individual segments, towards the outside chronological perimeter. Within this context, people may rise and fall, individually invoking the metaphor of Fortune and her wheel, but, when viewed over the scale of history, this rise and fall becomes a rational pattern paralleling an order of schematic retribution and, possibly, schematic reward. In this model, the wheel of Fortune is not fixed and spinning, but rolling forward, describing as it goes an undulating line that snakes its way towards the final 'restitution of things' or, within the specific temporal perimeters of the *Mirror*, the reign of Elizabeth: a cursus rather than a cycle. Scholars of Renaissance historiography have isolated Renaissance convictions that 'history is not the record of a random sequence of events but the record of a process, linear or cyclic or maybe even both, that defines the moral contour of events.'[28] Between its form and its content, *A Mirror for Magistrates* serves to demonstrate this 'even both,' bringing fortune and Providence together to describe what Sir Thomas Browne would later call a 'serpentine and crooked line.'[29]

Chapter Four

Women

While a great deal of work has been done in the past twenty years tracking the representation of women in the Renaissance, little attention has been paid to the depiction of women in de casibus tragedy.[1] When this literature has been related to the representation of women by critics such as Constance Jordan and Linda Woodbridge,[2] it has been seen either as a source for later material or as a form of 'lament' literature.[3] But I am going to argue that it was the form of this literature and its relation to history, more than its content (that is, the actual exempla of tragic protagonists), that should be examined as a site of gender politics, and that the adoption and subsequent manipulation of Boccaccio's form had ideological implications for the representation of political women.

In her book *Renaissance Feminism*, Constance Jordan outlines what she calls the 'terms of the debate' that informed the pro- and anti-woman publications of the sixteenth and seventeenth centuries. One of the terms Jordan lists is the 'literary representation of famous women,' and the seminal figure in this tradition was Boccaccio, who represented famous women in both *De casibus virorum illustrium* and *De mulieribus claris*.[4] Jordan is right to recognize Boccaccio's writing as misogynistic, but this misogyny comes through less in the actual representations of women that are presented in *De casibus* than in a famous digression against women in that book. That digression, which comes near the end of Book One, is the standard medieval and Renaissance anti-woman diatribe that 'the female of the species is very greedy, quick to anger, unfaithful, oversexed, truculent, desirous more of frivolity than of wisdom' (44). It is supported with a short list of duplicitous and greedy women, including Delilah, Iole, Clymenestra, and

Medea. Boccaccio makes the allures of women roughly analogous to the allures of fortune: they are both seductive and treacherous, but their dangers can be avoided by stoicism: 'No man can conquer others who has not first conquered himself. Therefore, if you will control the unrestrained passion which you have within you, then women will set their net and try their wiles in vain' (45). But he concedes that women can be good: 'for who does not believe that among so great a number you might find some who are dutiful, modest, very holy, and worthy of the highest respect? I will not mention Christian women who have a high reputation for magnanimity, integrity, virginity, simplicity, chastity, constancy, and other virtues, but some pagans who merit the highest praise' (45).

The actual stories of women in *De casibus* are less overtly anti-woman. Jocasta, Queen of Thebes, is treated as the remorseful victim of terrible circumstances. Dido, Queen of Carthage, is a chaste and resolute monarch. Zenobia, Queen of Palmyra, is a great and war-like ruler reduced by fortune. Cleopatra is a decadent seductress, but not presented without sympathy. The most obviously anti-woman tale is of Brunhildis, Queen of the Franks. Boccaccio argues with the spirit of this 'she-devil' about the facts of her life. Boccaccio accuses her repeatedly of lying ('I have known since I was boy that women have double tongues' [220]), of treachery, and of lasciviousness.

Boccaccio wrote *De mulieribus claris* in 1361 and revised it in 1362. Dedicated to Andrea Acciaiuoli, it relates the lives of famous pagan women, stressing, like Plutarch's *Mulierum virtutes*, the virtues of women. Like *De casibus*, it is sweeping in scope, covering lives from Eve to Queen Johanna of Naples. The work became associated, in the fifteenth century, with *De casibus*.[5] This association was as a history; the stories in *De mulieribus claris*, as in *De casibus*, are not called 'tragic' by Boccaccio, nor do they display a consistency of *metabasis*. There was an anonymous mid-fifteenth-century English verse translation of the book and a prose translation of forty-six of the lives made by Lord Morley, Henry Parker. The latter was written between 1534 and 1547, and dedicated to Henry VIII. Morley may have based his translation, as Lydgate did his of *De casibus*, on a French version by Laurent de Premierfait.[6]

Jordan has demonstrated how *De mulieribus claris*, while purporting to be an antidote to the Pauline tradition of silent and chaste womanhood, was in fact 'devious' in its rhetorical strategies, going on to depict 'women who appear to be more or less reprehensible, more or less ineffectual, or simply pathetic.'[7] Boccaccio's aim, Jordan argues, was to preserve *virtus* as masculine; women who ventured into the world of masculine prerogative were either vilified or came to a sticky end. Linda Woodbridge, on the other hand, sees Boccaccio's works as more important as a source of exempla for the later anti-feminist treaties of international humanists. These treaties, she argues, were formal exercises, 'intellectual calisthenics,' for a limited intellectual community, and should not be taken at their misogynistic face value.[8] Whatever the case, *De mulieribus claris* would not be very important in the English tradition of *de casibus* literature. Certainly, *De mulieribus claris* was known in England and advocated: Thomas Salter's 1579 instruction book for 'all Mothers, Matrones, and Maidens,' *The Mirrhor of Modestie*, recommended that women read the histories of women found in Boccaccio.[9] But Lydgate's translation, and the *Mirror*, made *De casibus* the better-known, more influential work.

Lydgate, in *Fall of Princes*, while purporting to be offering a fair and direct translation of *De casibus*, did take exception to Boccaccio's misogyny:

> But Bochas heer, I not what he doth meene,
> Maketh in his book an exclamacioun
> Ageyn[e]s women, that pite is to seene –
> Seith how ther lyne, ther generacioun
> Been off nature double off condicioun,
> And callith hem eek dyuers and onstable,
> Beestis rassemblyng that been insaciable.
>
> He meneth off women that be born in Crete,
> Nothyng off hem that duelle in this contre ...   (1: 4719–27)

When he translates the 'Against Women' passage, Lydgate counters Boccaccio's accusations by providing examples of good women to balance the examples of bad that Boccaccio provided. Distressed by Boccaccio's apparent misogyny – 'it doth my witt appall / Off this mateer to make rehersaile' (1: 6644–5) – Lydgate offers arguments by analogy to counter Boccaccio's sweeping condemnation of women: 'The riche rube nor the saphir ynde / Be nat appeired off ther fressh beute, / Though among stonys men countirfetis fynde' (6651–3). He concludes that only bad women, as only bad men, need fear the examples of *De casibus*:

Thouh Iohn Bochas in his opynyoun
Ageyn[es] women liset a processe make,
Thei that be goode off condicioun
Sholde ageyn hym no maner quarel take,
But lihtli passe, and ther sleuys shake.   (6700–4)

A Mirror for Magistrates contains no passages analogous to Boccaccio's diatribe against women. The longest direct discussion of gender politics comes in a prose link in the second part of the 1563 edition. After the tragedy of the rebellious Blacksmith, the contributors conclude that the tale proves 'to teach all people as well offycers as subiectes to consyder their estates and to lyue in loue and obedience to the hygheste powers' (1: 419). This leads to a defence of lineal succession, and a rebuttal of those realms who think it 'not meete for the feminine sexe to beare the royall office' (1: 419):

> so that the chiefest poynt of a princes offyce consysteth in obedience to god and to his ordynaunces, and what should let but that a woman may be as obedyent vnto god as a man? The second poynt of a princes offyce is to prouyde for the impotent, nedy, and helpless, as wydowes orphanes, lame and decrepite persons: And seing women are by nature tender harted, mylde, and pytefull, who maye better then they discharge this dutie? (1: 419–20)

When it is asserted that women lack the martial spirit necessary to be a successful monarch, arguments to the contrary are brought forward:

> *Debora, Iael, Iudith, Thomiris,* and other do proue the contrarye. But graunte it were so: what harme were that, seynge victorie consysteth not in wit or force, but in goddes good pleasure. I am sure that whatsoeuer prynce doth his dutie in obeying god, and causyng iustice to be mynistred according to gods lawes, shall not onelye lacke warre (be he man woman or chylde) But also be a terror to al other princes ... Mo warres haue ben sought through the wilful & hauty courages of kinges, and greater destruccions happened to realmes thereby, than by any other meanes. (1: 420)

The tradition of representing historical English women in *de casibus* tragedy began in the 1563 edition of the *Mirror*. It should have begun in the original 1559 edition, but at the last moment the tragedy of Elianor Cobham was delayed until the edition of 1578. So in the 1563

edition, the tale of 'Shore's Wife' by Thomas Churchyard was introduced.[10] It became the most popular story in the entire collection and
was variously treated after its publication up until the eighteenth century in ballads, plays, and finally operas.[11] Churchyard closely based
his story on the account of Jane Shore found in Sir Thomas More's *History of King Richard the thirde*,[12] an account that is repeated almost
exactly in Holinshed's *Chronicles*.[13] Shore, a low-born wife of a mercer,
was a famous beauty, and therefore came to the attention of King
Edward IV. He set her up as one of his mistresses; 'many he had, but
her he loued,' says More (56).[14] Once at court she was able to intercede
in the affairs of state, 'where the king toke displeasure, she would mit-
igate & appease his mind: where men were out of fauour, she wold
bring them in his grace. For many that had highly offended, shee
obtained pardon. Or great forfetures she gate men remission. And
finally in many weighty sutes, she stode many men in gret stede, either
for none, or very smal rewardes' (56). After Edward's death, Shore
became the mistress of Thomas Grey and became involved in the succession politics, acting as an agent of Lord Hastings. She was persecuted by Richard III, who made her perform public penance, had her
imprisoned, and then forced her to live as a beggar. Her plight, and
especially the spectacle of her penance, provoked great public interest.
She died in extreme poverty.

This story is not in line with the other tragedies in the early editions
of the *Mirror*. First, it is about a woman. Second, her tragedy does not
teach the clear political lesson in which the first contributors of the
Mirror were interested. Indeed, Churchyard makes Shore's story less
political than it in fact was. Shore is not presented in relation to any
political figures except Edward and Richard. Richard's proclamation
against her is not mentioned.[15] Her relationship with Lord Hastings is
not explained. Instead, the emphasis of the story is on the nature of
beauty and virtue, specifically chastity. The details that Churchyard
adds emphasize a personal, not a political, tragedy, with sentimental,
not political, consequences. And so Churchyard invents a forced and
unhappy marriage for Shore, a detail not in More. Her fall is used, not
to describe political vicissitudes, but to draw maxims about fickle Fortune: 'What greater gryefe may come to any lyfe, / Than after sweete
to taste the bitter sower?' (1: 382) Her final downfall is abrupt, and
except for mention of 'This raging wolfe' (1: 384) – Richard and his
vendetta – historical specifics are missing.

Compare this with the tragedy of Elianor Cobham, the second wife of Humphrey Duke of Gloucester, the second woman represented in this tradition (she was to have been the first). Her story could have been used to teach the dangers of lechery, for Cobham was first Humphrey's mistress, and their relationship was so scandalous that in 1428 a group of London housewives protested against it. But, instead, the story deals with Cobham's political manoeuvring to gain the throne for her husband, manoeuvres that involved astrology and witchcraft. In her tragedy, the ghost of Cobham traces the route of political infighting that brought about her fall and spends a great deal of time attacking her political opponent, Cardinal Beaufort (see, for example, 1: 438). As mentioned earlier, this story was suppressed until 1578, probably because of Duke Humphrey's reputation, and Lily B. Campbell has argued that the tragedy of Cobham is actually an allegory of the life of the young Queen Elizabeth.[16] The author of the story, George Ferrers, was an informant against the young Elizabeth to the Privy Council.

The prose envoy after the tragedy raises some interesting questions. First of all, the contributors discuss Cobham's poem as though it had been delivered by a real woman, even going on to discuss the verisimilitude of her having alluded to various myths:

> Sverly (sayd one of the companye) thys Lady hath don much to moue the hearers to pitye her, & hath very wel knyt vp the ende of her tragedy according to the beginning but I meruayle much where she learned al this Poetry touched in her tale, for in her dayes, learninge was not common, but a rare thinge, namely in women, yes (quod Maister Ferrers) that might she very wel learn of the Duke her Husbande, who was a Prince so excellently learned, as the like of his degree was no where to be founde. (1: 444)

Further, the contributors discuss the appropriateness of Cobham's vitriolic attack on her oppressors: 'Me thinke (quod another) she passeth bounds of a Ladies modesty, to inuey so cruelly agaynst the Cardinall Beaufort. Not a whit (quod another) hauing such cause as she had, & somewhat ye must beare with womens passions' (1: 444). The last comment is in line with the Renaissance perception of women as emotionally labile, but the excusing of Cobham because of the justness of her cause is unique in the collection: it suggests that women be allowed a voice, a political voice, if they are persecuted. They do not have to suffer in silence. Cobham's tale, then, was historically specific, relevant on two levels to contemporary politics, and unique in its portrayal of an actively political woman.

It was subsequently ignored. Shore's tale, not Cobham's, became the narrative paradigm into which all subsequent portrayals of women were made to fit in this tradition, or to be defined as being in opposition to. It set the pattern: a beautiful woman is tempted by sin (invariably lust), and incidentally power, and either succumbs, then dies, or resists then dies. Increasingly, as this literary tradition evolved, the women represented in this pattern belonged to legendary history, and so their stories, unlike Cobham's, could not be seen as having any direct significance in relation to contemporary politics. So, in the 1574 edition of the *Mirror*, written by John Higgins, we have the tragedies of Elstride; her daughter, Sabrine; and Cordila, which we discussed in the previous chapter. The title of the Elstride tragedy indicates the direction the representation of women in this tradition was now taking: 'Elstride the concubine of Locrinus myserably drowned by Gwendoline his wyfe, declares her presumption, lewde life and infortunate fall' (2: 87). In fact, the story contains little presumption or lewdness. The daughter of a German king drowned during an ill-fated campaign in England, Elstride, through circumstances beyond her control, ends up the concubine of King Locrinus. After Locrinus's death, Gwendoline, the queen, captures Elstride and her daughter, Sabrine, and, after much ranting and despite their pathetic pleas, has them both drowned. The tragedy of Sabrine tells the same story from the daughter's point of view. The story is that of the woman at the edges of power; the debate, however, is about chastity; the tone is one of pathos.

There is some movement back towards the political realm in the story of Cordila. In this version of the Lear story, Cordila returns from France to restore Lear to the throne, where he reigns for three years. Cordila then becomes queen and rules for five years, until her nephews, Morgan and Conidagus, the sons of Goneril and Regan, wage war on her. She is taken prisoner, and the contrast between former happiness and present sadness is worked out with much bad alliteration: 'From palace proude, in prison poore to lye: / From kingdomes twayne, to dungion one no more: / From Ladies wayting vnto vermine store' (2: 155). She finally kills herself, and it is the question of suicide, not the implications of her reign, that the poem ends up exploring.

Nevertheless, in seeming reaction against the very notion of a just and powerful woman, Thomas Blennerhasset, in the 1578 edition of the *Mirror*, presented the tragedy of Lady Ebbe, the narrative of which can be summarized by its title: 'Howe Lady Ebbe dyd flea her nose, and vpper lippe away, to saue her Virginitie' (2: 465). And not just her own nose: as an abbess, she convinced all of her nuns to mutilate themselves before the Danes sacked their nunnery. The nuns were not raped, but the Danes killed them: 'With fiery flames they burnt our Nunnery, / And vs therein: O wretched crueltie' (2: 468).

Part of this change in the representation of women can be explained by a shift in the *Mirror* itself as it went through subsequent editions. As we have seen, the early editions, those edited by Baldwin, were overtly political. The stories either had direct significance to the political concerns of the day (as with Edward Seymour) or underlined the need for honesty and altruism among political leaders. In these editions the stories of women were non-political; they dealt with questions of beauty and chastity. The one tragedy that depicted an actively political women was originally suppressed, then ignored. Later editions of the *Mirror*, and its imitations, moved away from potentially dangerous political censure; the sins they depicted in men were more likely to be moral than political. The stories were about drunkenness, lechery, avarice, and impiety among the mighty. In other words, sins against the body corporeal, not the body politic, were detailed, and the concatenation of the tales suggested a mechanical providence arrayed against moral turpitude rather than an avenging fate against political dishonesty.[17] In these later editions, women are depicted in particular situations that test their virtue, and are judged pure or lewd by their success at confronting this challenge, not by the moral conduct of their entire lives. In both cases the women's tales do not fit the dominant teleological pattern demonstrated by the repetition of the tragic narrative. Their stories may be tragic, but the significance of the tragedy is personal rather than public.

This exclusion took on a formal dimension as of 1591, for the success of 'Jane Shore' inspired other poets to write first-person non-dramatic tragedies of famous women, independent of the *de casibus* aggregate. But *de casibus* tragedy depends for its political/historical meaning on the teleology manifest in the narrative aggregate. To isolate the individual narrative is to dismiss it from the argument of history. This means that stories of historical women were formally excluded from the discussion of power. It became fashionable to attach a woman's tragedy not to a collection of historical poems, but to a sonnet sequence, a tradition not found in other 'mirrors' of historical men.[18]

Daniel's 'Rosamond' was attached to his sonnet sequence *Delia*

(1591) and was used as another device to win the poet's mistress's heart. The ghost of Rosamond says to the poet,

> *Delia* may hap to deigne to reade our Story,
> And offer vp her sighs among the rest,
> Whose merit would suffice for both our glory,
> Whereby thou might'st be grac'd and I be blest.   (82)[19]

The story of Rosamond is a remake of the tale of Shore's wife, with a dash of Elstride thrown in. Rosamond, a well-born, country-raised beauty, is ruined when she comes to Court. Once she becomes Henry II's concubine, he hides her from the Queen in a maze: 'here I inclos'd from all the world asunder, / The Minotaure of shame kept for disgrace' (98). The Queen eventually finds her and makes her drink poison. Rosamond dies alone and is mourned by the King.

In 1593, Thomas Lodge published a book titled *Phillis: Honoured with Pastorall Sonnets, Elegies, and amorous delights Where-vnto is annexed, the tragical complaynt of Elstred*. In it, he retells the Elstride story, but now as an adjunct to seduction, not as a political history. Also in 1593, Anthony Chute published his first work, *Beawtie dishonoured written vnder the title of Shores Wife*. This is a retelling of the Shore story for a more courtly audience. Chute blends allusions to Ovid with a more intense exploration of Shore's motivation.[20] So, while Shore's husband in the Thomas More history was 'an honest citezen, yonge & goodly & of good substance' (55), Chute describes him as a dotard: 'He could no more of loue, his dayes were don: / Crookt old, and cold' (sig. C2v).[21] Shore's power over the king, indeed her glory days at court, are reduced to a mere three lines: 'And this was commendably praysd in me, / That Sutor wrongs my selfe to right would bring / If right might be procured from the king' (sig. E2r). Notice the 'if': 'Chute implies that she only intervened in cases where success was assured.'[22] What small political power she has is entirely dependent on the King. Compare this to the original Churchyard: 'I governed him that ruled all this land: / I bare the sword though he did weare the crowne / I strake the stroke that threwe the mightye downe' (1: 379). Chute has depoliticized Shore to fit her new context as courtly entertainment.

The popularity of the Shore story, and its many imitators, prompted its original author, Churchyard, to reissue the poem in 1593: 'the Tragedie of Shores Wife, much augmented with diuers newe aditions.' It appeared in a book called *Churchyard's Challenge*, a miscellany to which Churchyard attached this statement in a prefatory note: 'because Rosimond is so excellently sette forth (the actor whereof I honour) I haue somewhat beautified my Shores wife, not in any kind of emulation, but to make the world knowe, my deuice in age is as ripe & reddie, as my disposition and knowledge was in youth' (126).[23] The beautification process entailed adding 169 new lines, platitudes about beauty and love, all conveniently marked with the standard flag of a double quotation mark in the margin. A third of these additions addresses the question of Shore's power at Court. While, in the original, Shore had ruled the King and used her power to good, utterly unselfish ends, in the new version Shore uses her power as a form of self-serving insurance: 'I did good turnes, whiles that I was a height: / For feare a flawe, of winde would make me reele, / And blowe me downe, when Fortune turnd her wheele' (135). So, when Churchyard returned to his poem, he updated it in accord with the trend in the representation of historical women in this tradition: he beautified, he qualified, he made decorative. He played down political activity in favour of sentiment, and he removed his heroine from the context of history.

Finally, in 1594, Drayton published 'Matilda: The faire and chaste Daughter of the Lord Robert Fizwater. The Trve Glorie of the Noble Hovse of Svssex.' Of all the poems in this tradition, 'Matilda' offers the most in the way of psychological exploration and dramatic irony, but its tone is overwhelmingly one of pathos.[24] The poem avoids any discussion of politics. Matilda's story is of a young, well-born woman whom King John wishes to take as a lover. She is enticed with the same power that Shore once exercised: 'Advaunce thy friends, and throw the mighty downe. / Be thou admir'd through all this famous Isle, / Thy name enrol'd with never-dated stile' (225).[25] But, Matilda's father asks, 'What Princes wealth can prize thy Maiden-head?' (222). She flees Court to a monastery, where she is confronted by an agent of the King, who says she must succumb to the King's lust or drink the poison he has brought. She does the latter, and dies thinking on 'My glorious life, my spotlesse Chastity' (240). The King is filled with remorse and pledges to make a pilgrimage to Matilda's tomb. Matilda is praised as a paragon of womanhood: chaste, passive, reclusive, attentive to her father, fleeing the offer of political power.

As Matilda flees the Court, so representations of women leave the aggregate, are excluded from the teleology of power. Women are consigned to the nunneries of sonnet sequences and miscellanies. This isolation is emphasized by intertextual reference. In the original Shore's wife, Shore's ghost says,

> And nowe a time for me I see preparde,
> I heare the lives and falles of many wyghtes:
> My tale therfore the better may be heard,
> For at the torche the litle candle lightes.
> Where Pageantes be, small thinges fil out the sightes.
> Wherefore geve eare, good Baldwyn do thy best,
> My tragedy to place among the rest.   (1: 375)

Her tragedy is to be placed in line with those of the men, although its significance is minimized through philophromesis.[26] By the time we get to Elstride, however, things have changed. Elstride's ghost begins, 'And must I needes my selfe resite my fall / Poore woman I? must I declare my fate?' (2: 87). Rather than seek a place in the pattern of history, she seeks to hide in shame, to scurry back to obscurity like the ghosts of the women in the underworld of Vergil's *Aeneid*. And by the time of the independent tragedies the ghosts are in direct competition with each other, not with men. When the ghosts of these women speak, they do not relate themselves to the tides of history, but rather to the tales of other women. This is clearest in 'Matilda.' That ghost mentions the famous women treated to date: Rosamond, Lucrece, Shore, and Elstride, and concludes, 'Thus looser wantons, still are praisd of many, / Vice oft findes friends, but vertue seldom any' (1: 215). She does not mention Cobham or Cordila, women who wielded real political power. The historical women are relegated to their own debate on a single subject, chastity, that quality which much of the popular press in the sixteenth century argued was women's only virtue.[27]

One more formal device of this tradition should be noted. In the English *de casibus* tradition, the tales are all putative autobiographies addressed by the ghost to the recording poet. They are first-person narratives delivered, often in a vision, to the writer. The poet plays both character and audience, both deceased, lamenting woman, and living, recording man. The poet grants both voice and text to the woman, and that text is history itself. As the women in these stories are dependent upon men for whatever political power they wield, so are their fictive ghosts dependent upon men for articulation. So Daniel's Rosamond says to the poet

Then write ... the ruine of my youth,
Report the downe-fall of my slippry state:
Of all my life reueale the simple truth,
To teach to others what I learnt too late.
Exemplifie my frailtie, tell how Fate
  Keepes in eternall darke out fortunes hidden,
  And ere they come to know them tis forbidden.   (83)

The female ghosts plead with the male poets to be allowed a place in history, a request that is, as we have seen, rarely granted.

But what happens when the poet/historian is confronted with the example of a powerful woman whose history cannot be reduced to a parable of chastity? which will not fit the Shore paradigm? The form fails. The tradition affords two examples. The first is the legendary Queen Hellina, who is treated in the 1578 *Mirror for Magistrates*. Hellina was the English mother of Constantine the Great and the ruler who brought Christianity to England. The title of her tale indicates how far from the *de casibus* form her story is: 'How Queene Hellina was Empresse of all the Worlde. This Storie dooth declare how happye they bee, which liue in the feare and loue of God' (2: 412). In the prose introduction to the poem, the character Inquisition laments the fact that 'the descriptions of time, I meane the Chronicles, haue lefte so litle reporte of her, that I founde her standyng betwixte *Forgetfulnesse* and *Memory*, almost smothered with *Obliuion*' (2: 411). The character of Memory, when first presented with Hellina, mistakes her for the goddess Diana. Her story is not a tragedy, but a Christian comedy which ends with 'Euen in this blesse a better blesse befel, / I dyde, and nowe my soule in heauen doth dwel' (2: 420). It reads like a first-person version of the idealized eulogies of women that were popular in the English Renaissance, a literary form that Retha M. Warnicke has argued was 'an integral part of the gender socialization process' of the age.[28]

Hellina remains in the aggregate, but not within the defining narrative trope. Similarly, it proves harder to appropriate her voice. Her opening words are not a plea, but a command and a surprising acknowledgment of the patriarchal control of history:

Mens due desertes ech Reader may recite,
For men of men doo make a goodly show,
But womens workes can neuer come to light,
No mortall man their famous factes may no:

No writer wull a litle time bestowe,
The worthy workes of women to repeate,
Though their renowme and due deserts be great.   (2: 412)

But the 'worthy workes' of her life offer no threat to the teleology of the form. Hellina is depicted as submitting to a series of men. When the Roman emperor Constantinus asks for her hand in marriage, she grants it only after seeking the advice of her male council. After the Emperor dies, and the son, Constantine, proves himself in battle, Constantine says that the empire belongs to his mother, but Hellina turns it down: 'I am content to liue with lesse degree. / O louing sonnee geue eare vnto my hest, / I wyl not rule, that charge for thee is best' (2: 420).

But this tradition fails entirely before the great example that counterbalances it: Queen Elizabeth herself. If the formal strategies I have outlined served to imply the historical inevitability of patriarchalism, they were confounded by the example of the defining figure of the age in which most of them were written. The irony is manifest in 'England's Eliza,' written by Richard Niccols for the 1610 version of *A Mirror for Magistrates*. In it the spirit of Elizabeth comes to the poet as he sits dreaming near the Thames, exhausted by his melancholy, musing on the glories of his late Queen. Elizabeth appears to him at the head of the nine muses (780). The tale, like that of Hellina, is a comedy, and therefore does not fit the defining narrative of *de casibus* tragedy. Even more – we are told that 'Fortune, as loth so rare a worked to spill, / At our Great Britaine maid did not repine, / But did to her all happinesse assigne' (786). The rise and fall of history stops; the defining tragic pattern does not, cannot, apply. The teleology of history altered to accommodate the late Queen. And the first-person device is abandoned before Elizabeth. The poet dares not appropriate her voice, so her story is told in the third person by Clio, the muse of history, who herself is reluctant to tell the story: 'Would God (quoth shee) her prayses I could speak, / Who claimes a greater power her praise to found, / Then Phoebus self, if greater could be found' (782). The historical fact of Elizabeth's reign undermined any formal attempt to isolate women from the teleology of history. The form that could not accommodate her example destroyed itself in an attempt at closure. It ended denying its own terms. Historical fact could not be marginalized by this strategy of historical representation. *De casibus* tragedy petered out, and the *Mirror*'s last edition did not sell. The case of Elizabeth exemplified the frailty of a form that excluded the powerful women of history.

Chapter Five

Drama

As mentioned in the introduction, the bulk of the scholarship on *A Mirror for Magistrates* and the *de casibus* tradition has been done by critics exploring the background of Elizabethan drama. The *de casibus* tradition has been seen, at best, as a stepping stone in the evolution of tragedy, a sort of lamentable missing link on the way to *true* tragedy – the works of Kyd, Marlowe, and, above all, Shakespeare – despite the fact that critics such as Sidney grouped the *Mirror* with dramatic tragedies.[1] For this reason, the scholarship that exists on the *Mirror* is, for the most part, furtive; critics dig in the book to find the passages that dramatists have used in their plays, then hurry away. No one has thought to reverse the process and ask what the *Mirror* used from drama. This is the first question this chapter will address.

The second question this chapter will pose is a variation on an old scholarly paradigm: looking at the influence the *Mirror* had on drama, not as a source of historical anecdote, though, but as a form of popular-history writing. In other words, we will examine the impact that the *de casibus* form, as it has been defined in these pages, had on the dramatic representation of history. Rather than assume that dramatists mined the *de casibus* texts for exempla, let us look at how the dramatists' practice was informed by the narrative tropes of historical representation that the *Mirror* popularized. This raises a series of new questions about the relationship between the texts, questions involving not only conceptions of historical form, but popular perceptions of history, the nature of historical character, and historical literacy.

The *Mirror* is related to drama through its writers and cultural context. As we noted at the outset, Baldwin worked on plays and pastimes for the Court Christmas season in 1552–3. Thomas Sackville, author of the 'Induction,' which would become the most critically acclaimed piece of writing in the *Mirror*'s long publishing history, was a dramatist. He wrote, along with Thomas Norton, the seminal dramatic tragedy *Gorboduc; Or, Ferrex and Porrex*, which was played both at the Inner Temple and before the Queen at Whitehall Palace. George Ferrers, a major contributor to the Baldwin editions, was lord of misrule at Court under both Henry VIII and Edward. The number of contributors involved in dramatic ventures is not surprising: the *Mirror* was published in those decades that saw the rise of the professional player (it was first published in 1559, the year that Warwick's Men became active), and the construction of the first permanent theatres in England.

Indeed, there is something dramatic, or, rather, theatrical, about the process of composition of the Baldwin editions of the *Mirror*. As we saw in chapter 2, the early editions of the *Mirror* combined the authority of the exemplary mode with the authority of the collective voices of citizen authors. Both the collective nature of authors' endeavour and its intention, to shape the chronicle histories into a series of monologues, should remind us of professional theatrical enterprise in late Tudor London. Michael Bristol, using the critical language of Mikhail Bakhtin, describes the public playhouses of late Elizabethan London this way:

> The playhouse is not simply a theatre in which a literary heteroglossia is performed, but an actual heteroglot institution in which the exchange of experience crosses every social boundary, and the diversity of speech types traverses the genres of literature and of authoritative discourse.
> This is cultural activity mandated by a 'dialogic imperative' rather than by any prior allocation and structuring of authority.[2]

This is, with some modification, a good description of Baldwin's *Mirror*. His writers' collective was a heteroglot organization that produced a heteroglossic text. While the *Mirror* does not incorporate the diversity of speech types that we associate with much of the public drama of the age, within the strict parameters of the exemplary mode it was remarkably eclectic. And, like the theatre, its activity was authorized by 'dialogic imperative,' the praxis of articulation. It presented itself as a social project (in the prose links) that used a virtual present (the process of composition as it is recorded in the links) to expound the past in first-person speech. Some eight years before the first permanent theatre, the Red Lion, was built near London, the *Mirror* prefigured many Elizabethan theatrical practices.

It may have been a confluence of dramatic energy, then, rather than a peek at the manuscript of Cavendish's *Metrical Visions*, that inspired Baldwin (and perhaps, independently, Cavendish) to make the major change that he introduced to the *de casibus* formula: having the ghosts speak in the first person rather than being, as they are in almost all of Boccaccio, spoken for after the fact by the narrator. This change made the *Mirror* inherently dramatic; the book may be considered a collection of soliloquies. And, while in most cases the dramatic potential of the form was not overtly acknowledged, there are moments in which the contributors make gestures at the tradition of theatrical representation. When the writers take the time to describe the ghost who is about to speak, they are attaching an image of a body to the voice, creating a character, implying an actor: 'For the better perceyuing whereof, you must ymagin that you se him a meruaylous wel fauoured man, holdinge in his hand, his owne hart, newely ripped out of his brest, and smoking forth the lively spirit: and with his other hand, beckening to and fro, as it were to warne vs to auoyde: and with his faynte tounge and voyce, sayeng as coragiously as he may, these wordes that folowe' (1: 346). Sometimes, a specific scene is described for the ghost, so we have an idea of a setting, a stage. In the prose link before the tragedy of Richard Plantagenet that appears in Baldwin's 1563 edition, the author says, 'for the better vnderstanding whereof, imagine that you see him tormented with Dives in the diepe pit of Hell, and thence howlinge this that foloweth' (1: 359).

There is also some movement towards dramatic characterization through language. While most of the poems in the collection do not contain anything approaching a manifestation of personality through poetry, instead using an undifferentiated language of political and historical didacticism for all the characters, there are moments in the books that point towards an awareness of the potential of language to embody character in a way that is inherently dramatic. And if, as we suggested in chapter 2, the exemplary mode's authority rests, in part, upon the reader identifying with the protagonist of the exemplum, then the creation of characters naturalistic enough to be sympathetic increases the political potential of the text. So the *Mirror* authors, concerned with the decorum of character representation, discuss the appropriateness of the various ghosts' speeches. After the tragedy of Richard, Duke of Gloucester, one of Baldwin's collaborators complains: 'It is not meete that so disorderly and vnnatural a man as kyng Richard was, shuld observe any metrical order in his talke' (1: 371); poetic form should accord with personality. The group agrees, but rather than recast the tragedy, they push on to the next story. In the prose link after the tragedy of the Blacksmith, a collaborator raises a technical objection: 'It is pitie (quoth one) that the meter is no better seing the matter is so good.' But, he is told, 'the Author him selfe ... could haue doen that, but he woulde not, and hath desyred me that it maye passe in suche rude sorte as you haue heard it: for he obserueth therein a double *decorum* both of the Smyth, and of him selfe: for he thinketh it not mete for the Smyth to speke, nor for himselfe to write in any exacte kynde of meter' (1: 419). The extremes of this are the admittedly heavy-handed attempts at the representation of personality that call upon a medieval tradition of vice figures. These are found throughout the later editions of the text. So, the tragedy of King Iago who died of lethargy begins,

> Haue I oreslept my selfe, or am I awake?
> Or hadst thou late oreslept thy selfe that wrote?
> Could'st thou not for the Letharge paynes to take:
> And with the rest his sleepy life to note?
> Was I amongst the wicked wights forgote?
> Well then, awaked sith wee are both twayne,
> To write my sleepy sinfull life, take payne.   (2: 236)

And while the monologues of the ghosts are the obvious examples of quasi-dramatic representation in the *Mirror*, we should remember that the prose links in the Baldwin editions can also be considered 'dramatic' in their representation of dialogue and the re-creation of collective endeavour. So, for example, we have this exchange in the prose link before Sackville's 'Induction':

> Then sayd the reader: The next here whom I finde miserable are king Edwards two sonnes, cruelly murdered n the tower of London: Haue you theyr tragedy? No surely (quoth I) The Lord Vaulx vndertooke to penne it, but what he hath done therein I am not certayne, & therfore I let it pass til I know farder. I haue here the duke of Buckingham, king Richardes chyefe instrument, wrytten by mayster Thomas Sackuille. Read it we pray you sayd they; with a good wyl (quoth I) but fyrst you shal heare his preface or Induction. (1: 297)

And at times the links present a narrative of the writers themselves. In the long prose link after the story of Jack Cade, Baldwin tells us that, while the assembled writers perused the Chronicles, 'I was so wearye that I waxed drowsye, and began in dede to slumber: but my imaginacion styll prosecutyng this tragicall matter, brought me suche a fantasy. me thought there stode before vs, a tall mans body full of fresshe woundes, but lackyng a head' (1: 181). This leads to the story of Richard, Duke of York, after which Baldwin says, 'With this, mayster *Ferrers* shooke me by the sleve, saying: why how now man, do you forget your selfe? belike you mind our matters very much: So I do in dede (quoth I) For I dreame of them' (1: 191). Baldwin is making a rudimentary closet drama of the process of the *Mirror*'s authorship, framing the ghostly monologues with the dialogue of their creator, creators who, incidentally, are also an audience to whom the ghosts complain ('Beware, take heede, take heede, beware, beware / You Poetes you' [1: 347]) and who pass judgment on the virtues of the tragedy they have just heard.

But there is little in the way of direct reference to dramatic tragedy in the *Mirror*, and most of what appears seems to be conventional metaphor rather than an engagement with theatrical tradition. So, in the third tragedy of the 1559 edition, Thomas, Duke of Gloucester, says,

> Thus hoysted so high on Fortunes wheele,
> As one on a stage attendyng a playe,
> Seeth not on whiche syde the scaffolde doth reele,
> Tyll tymber and poales, and all flee awaye:
> So fared it by mee, for day by daye   (1: 94)

Similarly, Henry, Duke of Buckingham tells us,

> In place of whom, as it befel my lot,
> Like on a stage, so stept I in strayt waye,
> Enioying there but wofully go wot,
> As he that had a slender part to playe:
> To teache therby, in earth no state may stay,
> But as our partes abridge or length our age
> So passe we all while others fyll the stage.   (1: 319)

Perhaps the most direct reference comes in Higgins's edition of 1587 in the tragedy of King Forrex:

Complayne I may with tragiques on the stage,
Compeld I am amongst the rest that fell:
I may complayne that felt of warres the wage,
Vntimely death I drewe, doth mee compell.   (2: 240)

This may be a reference to Sackville and his play *Gorboduc*, which features the history of Forrex.

Let us now turn to the question of the influence that the *de casibus* tradition, especially the *Mirror*, had on Elizabethan drama. But rather than look for allusions to the stories of the *Mirror* in specific plays, let us trace the impact that the *de casibus* narrative of history had on drama. To do this with any comprehensiveness would require a separate book, so I would like here to initiate this project by offering a short overview of the relation between *de casibus* literature and the most famous history plays ever written – Shakespeare's. After suggesting some ways in which this connection might be explored, I will offer a more detailed study of *Richard II* as a sort of critical test case.

Shakespeare's first history plays, *1*, *2*, and *3 Henry VI*, covered approximately the same historical period as the first Baldwin edition of the *Mirror*. Geoffrey Bullough, in his *Narrative and Dramatic Sources of Shakespeare*, lists parts of the *Mirror* as analogues, if not direct sources, for the *Henry VI* plays, but he admits that almost all the *Mirror* might be so cited.[3] It is tempting to postulate, from this parallel, that Shakespeare turned to writing history plays on the basis of the popularity of the *Mirror* and that he modelled his dramas on that bestselling history. However, this may be to overreach: the Wars of the Roses were of general interest in Shakespeare's time and had been treated in other places. They are prominent, of course, in Shakespeare's primary sources: Edward Hall's *The Union of the Two Noble Famelies of Lancastre and Yorke* (1548), Holinshed's *The Third Volume of Chronicles* (1587), and Book Eight of Geoffrey of Monmouth's *Historia regum britanniae*. There had been previous dramatic treatments of the reigns of several of the kings that Shakespeare represents in his tetralogy. It might be safer to speculate that both Baldwin and Shakespeare were drawn to represent this period of English history for at least four possible reasons: first, it was being treated in the Chronicles and other literature, and therefore source material was readily available; second, the previous treatments indicated that the material was popular; third, as we have already seen in relation to the publishing history of the *Mirror*, the period still had political implications for the present and was, therefore, topical; fourth, and this is admittedly more speculative, there was no period of English history that more easily fit the *de casibus* pattern. Baldwin, when looking to extend *Fall of Princes*, could have found no segment of English history that more clearly illustrated Boccaccio's narrative trope. Shakespeare, if he was thinking, at least in the first years of his career, of history in a *de casibus* format, would also have been drawn to this tumultuous period of English dynastic struggle.

Whatever the case, there is good reason to call these early plays of Shakespeare's, not history plays or, as they have been termed more recently by critics such as Phyllis Rackin, chronicle plays, but, rather, *de casibus* plays, if we use the definition of *de casibus* literature that I have outlined here. That is because these plays, especially the three *Henry VI* plays but also, in different ways, *Henry VIII* and *Richard II*, represent in dramatic format the vision of history that *de casibus* literature offers in its concatenation of tragic biographies. History, in these plays, is a ceaseless pattern of rising and falling fortunes; men and women, both good and bad, are destroyed in either obviously providential or simply arbitrary ways. The focus in these plays is not on the individual, but on the pattern that their successive fates describes.

It would be surprisingly if this were not so. Shakespeare could not but have been familiar with the *de casibus* formula. When he began to write history, he would have had the popular understanding of history as tragic. He had, almost certainly, read the *Mirror*. It would have been natural for him to try to write plays that followed the historical-literary formula with which both he and his audience were familiar. So what we have in the first tetralogy and the beginning of the second is a dramatic rendering of material that followed, as much as was possible in a drama, the *de casibus* model. Over the course of his career of writing history plays, Shakespeare moved away from the *de casibus* formula, both because the form becomes dated and unpopular, and because Shakespeare invented new ways of delivering historical material in compelling dramatic narratives.

The *de casibus* nature of the world of *Henry VI* is apparent from the outset of that play. We are not given a vision of history in which great individuals act as the prime movers in large events. The king, in these plays, is not a defining centre of historical meaning. Indeed, as Alexander Leggatt has pointed out, 'the first half of 1 *Henry VI*, like the Roman plays, is set in a kingless world.'[4] This refusal to focus on the monarch continues in the other plays: in 2 *Henry VI* the king is ineffective, manipulated by a myriad of conflicting forces; in 3 *Henry VI* he is deposed, imprisoned, and finally murdered, yet not even these moments of paramount dynastic importance are the centre of stage attention for very long. No, the *Henry VI* plays are not about the fall of the king; they are, like *de casibus* literature, about the falls of *many* people. The deaths begin in 1 *Henry 6* in 1.4, when the Earl of Salisbury and Sir Thomas Gargrave are killed by a French sniper as they stand with Talbot, reviewing the fortifications of Orleans. The unexpectedness of their deaths – they are cut down just as they are planning their assault on the French town – prepares us for a world much different from that of classical tragedy. This is a world in which death may strike providentially or arbitrarily, a world in which any great personage's death is a synecdoche for the tragic pattern of history. Talbot's address to the dying Salisbury suggests that this is something the soldier understands: '"How far'st thou, mirror of all martial men? / One of thy eyes and thy cheek's side stuck off? / Accursèd tower! Accursèd fatal hand that / That hath contrived this woeful tragedy"' (1.4.74–7).[5] And, indeed, the deaths continue. In 4.7 Talbot and his son die.

In 2 *Henry VI*, the *de casibus* pattern begins to become more clear as sad stories accumulate. We are presented with the downfall of Humphrey, Duke of Gloucester, and the humiliation of his wife (material that, as we have seen, was cut from the first edition of the *Mirror*, and later printed in the 1578 edition). We see Jack Cade's rebellion and its murderous chaos, and the falls of the Duke of Suffolk and Cardinal Winchester. Matthew Gough 'and all the rest' are slain in 4.7, Cade is finally killed in 4.10, and old Clifford dies in fight with York in the last act. This impressive number of deaths is framed by prophecy, a recurrent concern in the play epitomized in 1.4, when Eleanor Cobham, the Duchess of Gloucester, conjures a demon to foretell the political future. As David Bevington has argued, 'prophecy ... serves not to allow human beings to escape their destiny, which is unavoidable, but to give them the opportunity to perceive at last the pattern of divine justice. The audience realizes that prophecy is a divine warning too often unheeded by foolish human beings, and acknowledges the necessity of a fulfilment that is tragic and dispiriting but also comforting to the extent that it shows the heavens to be just.'[6] What Bevington does not note is that the pattern is one that would have been familiar to the audience: it is the *de casibus* pattern of rise and fall. None of the prophecies that Cobham receives from the demon is of riches and happiness;

they all foretell or imply the death and destruction we would expect in a *de casibus* world.

The play *3 Henry VI* most clearly follows a *de casibus* model. If we could argue that the first two plays are bound by the titular king, or at least by those few who were working around him, that cannot be said of the third play, in which kings come and go. Indeed, the relentlessly bloody action of the play marks it as, perhaps, the most *de casibus* of all Shakespeare's plays and may go some way towards explaining its lack of popularity in modern times. The parade of death begins in 1.1, when the head of Somerset is brought on stage. The child Rutland is killed by Clifford in 1.3; Queen Margaret kills York in 1.4. In 2.5, a son is killed by his father and a father killed by his son. In 2.6, Clifford dies with an arrow in his neck. In 5.2, Warwick dies with a *de contemptu mundi* oration on his lips that could be placed in any of the *Mirror*'s soliloquies:

> Lo, now my glory smeared in dust and blood!
> My parks, my walks, my manors that I had,
> Even now forsake me, and of all my lands
> Is nothing left me but my body's length.
> Why, what is pomp, rule, reign, but earth and dust?
> And, live we how we can, yet die we must.   (5.2.23–8)

Prince Edward dies at the hands of King Edward and Richard Gloucester in 5.5, and King Henry is stabbed by Gloucester in the next scene while he prophesies what that man will become. If this catalogue of catastrophe were not enough to mark the play as a dramatic rendering of the *de casibus* compendium of sad stories, references to fortune, such as King Edward's declaration 'Though Fortune's malice overthrow my state, / My mind exceeds the compass of her wheel' (4.3.46–7), and the oscillating successes of Edward and Henry, put that historical model firmly in mind.

What we see, then, in the *Henry VI* plays, is a *de casibus* pattern. This goes some way towards explaining the ambiguous or tragic endings of those plays. These plays do not promise, at their closings, that peace will be restored; they imply that the cycle of rising and falling action will continue into the foreseeable future. But the *de casibus* pattern breaks in *Richard III*. While the play as a whole may be read as a sort of ironic comment on the last line of *3 Henry VI* – 'For here, I hope, begins our lasting joy' (5.7.46) – that implies a continuation of the *de casibus* formula until the reign of Elizabeth, in this play Shakespeare moves away from drama that is dependent upon a *de casibus* formula by focusing so heavily on the lead character that the nearest literary form that can be invoked is classical, specifically Senecan, tragedy. While there continues to be sad stories, lives of great men reduced, the pattern is a background to the main story of Richard. Shakespeare, focusing all his attention on one character, the great bugaboo of Tudor history, draws on dramatic traditions rather than historiographic ones, bringing in the Vice figure from morality drama and the stage Machiavel popularized by Christopher Marlowe in *The Jew of Malta*. The play ends, unlike the *Henry VI* plays, with an unalloyed triumph, the beginning of a new dynasty that will result in the reign of Elizabeth.

If Shakespeare moves away from the *de casibus* formula towards the end of his first tetralogy, he returns to it at the beginning of his second. There are two possible reasons for this. First, *Richard II* depicts the earliest history in the eight plays that make up the two tetralogies. The reign of Richard leads to the civil wars of the *Henry IV* plays, the triumphs of *Henry V*, the dynastic chaos of the *Henry VI*, and finally the terror of the reign of Richard III. Introducing the *de casibus* formula at the chronological, if not compositional, beginning of this cycle gives the entire corpus a literary template.

On the other hand, the plays that Shakespeare writes after *Richard II*, *Henry IV* and *Henry V*, use much less of the formal structure of *de casibus* literature than the plays of the first tetralogy. While *Henry IV* does depict some sad stories, notably the fall of Hotspur in Part 1 and the fall (though not death) of Falstaff in Part 2, the action in both of these plays is articulated in a bifold structure that parallels the political story line with the tale of Hal and his adventures in the tavern, rather than the accumulative structure that we find in the *Henry VI* plays, especially Part 3. *Richard II*, then, serves as Shakespeare's departure from the *de casibus* formula that he employed in the first tetralogy. And indeed, as we shall see, the play does not so much body forth the *de casibus* structure in its own form as reflect upon it. This makes sense: Richard II is the most poetic of Shakespeare's monarchs; he, unlike the other kings Shakespeare put on the stage, understands the *de casibus* pattern because he has read the *Mirror*.

But the last history play that Shakespeare wrote, or co-wrote with John Fletcher, *The Life of King Henry VIII*, returns to a large degree to the *de casibus* formula. The king, while more prominent than Henry VI in his eponymous plays, is largely a bureaucrat who manifests true regal power only near the end of the play. The play is not structured around him, but rather around a series of falls of great people: the Duke of Buckingham, Queen Katherine, and Cardinal Wolsey. This pattern is anticipated by the prologue, whose injunction to the audience would not have been out of place in the *Mirror*:

> Think you see them great,
> And followed with the general throng and sweat
> Of thousand friends; then, in a moment, see
> How soon this mightiness meets misery.   (27–30)

The very first scene of the play works out the *de casibus* instability of fortune in miniature. Buckingham is complaining to the Duke of Norfolk about Wolsey, 'this holy fox,' whom he is about to charge with corruption and treason. In the very midst of these accusations, Buckingham is himself arrested, on trumped-up charges initiated by Wolsey, and by 2.1 Buckingham is being led to his execution with newly discovered humility: 'When I came hither, I was Lord High Constable / And Duke of Buckingham; now, poor Edward Bohun' (102–3). His fate and final oration reach for heights of sentimentality. Understanding the tragic empathy needed, a bystander to Buckingham's last speech declares, 'O, this is full of pity!' (2.1.136). Queen Katherine's fall from grace, again engineered by Wolsey, is similarly designed to tug at the heart strings. She is given long speeches at her trial (2.4), in conversation with Wolsey (3.1), and in the sickness that leads to her death (4.2), that combine protestations of innocence with, eventually, a reluctant acceptance of her undeserved deposition. This acceptance of her place in history, like that of Queen Hellina in the *Mirror*, earns her eternal life, presaged by a vision of heavenly reward (4.2.82ff). Wolsey's fall is the most dramatic, protracted, and didactic of the three. As soon as he senses the king's disfavour, Wolsey predicts his future: 'I have touched the highest point of all my greatness, / And, from that full meridian of my glory / I haste now to my setting' (3.2.224–6). After his fall, Wolsey delivers a soliloquy that draws, in the best *Mirror* tradition, a universal pattern together with his individual case:

> This is the state of man: today he puts forth
> The tender leaves of hopes; tomorrow blossoms,
> And bears his blushing honors thick upon him;
> The third day comes a frost, a killing frost,
> And when he thinks, good easy man, full surely

His greatness is a-ripening, nips his root,
And then he falls as I do. I have ventured,
Like little wanton boys that swim on bladders,
This many summers in a sea of glory,
But far beyond my depth.   (3.2.353–62)

He dies humbled, with hopes of heaven.

The *de casibus* pattern implicit in the action of *Henry VIII*, like that in the *Mirror* itself, ends in a vision of the reign of Queen Elizabeth. As Niccols, in *England's Eliza*, envisioned a reign in which the rise-and-fall pattern of history was frozen at a peak, in which Fortune ceased to turn her wheel about, so Shakespeare ends his last history play with the prophesy of Thomas Cranmer: 'In her days every man shall eat in safety / Under his own vine what he plants, and sing / The merry songs of peace to all his neighbors' (5.5.34–6). Shakespeare goes Niccols one better, extending this vision of peace to her successor, James I, the monarch at the time that Shakespeare wrote this play: 'He shall flourish, / And like a mountain cedar reach his branches / To all the plains about him' (5.5.53–5).

Before turning to a more detailed examination of *Richard II*, we may want to speculate that one of the reasons that the popularity of the *de casibus* structure, and the *Mirror* itself, declined in the early seventeenth century is that Shakespeare and other dramatists had been offering the public, since at least the 1590s, a new form of popular history, one that even the illiterate could enjoy. These new narratives of history, new tropes of historical discourse, supplanted the exemplary mode of *de casibus* with a model based, not on concatenation, but on the complex interaction of historical subjects and institutional structures. Such a model, exemplified in the *Henry IV* plays and *Henry V*, may have spoken more directly to the urban populace of the late sixteenth and early seventeenth centuries than the *de casibus* form, for this was the period in which the citizenry were actively redefining themselves in the face of institutional inertia and class hostility.

If we tie the rise in the popularity of drama, especially history drama, to the specific publishing history of the *Mirror*, other possibilities emerge. As Phyllis Rackin has argued, history was increasingly an area of general interest and speculation in late sixteenth-century England. The popularity of Shakespeare's drama was, she argues, in part due to the fact that it offered multivocal renditions of historical circumstance, through the 'polyphonic form of theatrical performance,' that qualified and questioned the apparently monologic chronicle histories that 'obscured the differences between the disparate authorial voices, opposed discursive positions, divergent accounts, and contradictory interpretations that were incorporated into the historiographic text.'[7] They did this by disguising their own complex authorship histories and convoluted use of sources behind simple, univocal author names, such as Hall or Holinshed, and texts that did not acknowledge opposition or divergence of accounts in their narratives.[8]

But, as we have seen, the Baldwin editions of the *Mirror* were themselves polyphonic and, unlike the large chronicle histories of the age, did not hide the trials of multiple authorship. If Rackin is correct in her assertion that Shakespeare's history plays were popular, in part, because their multivocal subversion of historical hegemony resonated for a heterogenous audience of increasing historical sophistication, might not the same be said of the Baldwin editions of the *Mirror*? It may be that, as the *Mirror* was taken over by the later editors, and ceased to offer such complexities, its audience turned away from it and towards the drama that offered analogous, heteroglossic narratives of history. This is not to say that Shakespeare and other dramatists copied the *Mirror*, but, rather, that they took over a function that the *Mirror* instituted, then abandoned: the representation of English history in a format that emphasized its instability and its dependency upon the interpretation of sources, and therefore drew attention to the ideological constructedness of history itself.

Let us now turn to *Richard II*, a play that seems, in many ways, to be Shakespeare's meditation on the *de casibus* form. At the beginning of the play, the King returns from Ireland to be confronted with the news of his troops' desertion and the death of his supporters, Bushy, Greene, and the Earl of Wiltshire. Richard's reaction is to sink on the beach in a self-indulgent funk:

> For God's sake let us sit upon the ground
> And tell sad stories of the death of kings:
> How some have been depos'd, some slain in war,
> Some haunted by the ghosts they have deposed,
> Some poisoned by their wives, some sleeping kill'd,
> All murthered – (3.2.155–60)[9]

Footnotes point out the allusion here to the 'medieval' Christian tradition of *de casibus* tragedy and move on,[10] but we recognize that Richard is summoning a narrative aggregate that will prove the tragic nature of history, and therefore validate his own experience. This tragic teleology, proven by a massive concatenation of biographies, is what we mean by the *de casibus* form.

When Shakespeare has Richard invoke 'sad stories,' then, he is tapping a popular concept of the process of history: virtually all kings die tragically; Richard will too. A tragic metabasis dominates history; Richard's story is one more proof of this teleology. Shakespeare will hint at this pattern over the whole course of the Henriad. As Richard sees himself as one example of a pre-existing pattern, within the plays he introduces the pattern; his fall dominates the Henriad as surely as his coffin dominates the last scene of his play. The beleaguered Henry IV, Hotspur, and Falstaff all add their sad stories after Richard's. If we take both of Shakespeare's tetralogies and run them together in chronological order, we find a macroscopic rise-and-fall pattern, from Richard II, through Henry V, and down to Richard III, that itself may be described as *de casibus*.

What I would like to emphasize here, though, is that this model of history determines the nature of the representation of historical character in the play. When Richard invokes the *de casibus* precedent, he is moving towards a construction of an historical self around a popular vision of the form of history. To use Marshall Grossman's term, he is a 'self-authored subject':

> The self-authored subject ... accumulates experiences through a series of judgments and choices that extend over the period of its life. As a fully historical conception of the self, it faces the problem of changing in response to temporally unfolding events while maintaining an essential continuity with its own past. Self-authorship, therefore, may be understood as the temporal recuperation of the tension between the self-fashioning and self-cancellation – the alternating experience of oneself as mastering and mastered – described by [Stephen] Greenblatt.[11]

However, the represented self maintains a continuity, in this play, not to the facts of history, but to the perceived *shape* of history. The 'historical' King Richard, as he was known to Shakespeare through his study of Holinshed and other sources, is not of primary significance here for two reasons: first, because Shakespeare changed the facts of the story; and, second, because it is not clear how much the audience knew of the historical past of Richard.

This second point raises problems. There seems to be a consensus on the part of many critics of Shakespeare's history plays that Shakespeare's audience not only knew their history, but also had sufficient historical knowledge to be able to spot anachronisms: they knew the real age of Richard's wife, that benevolences were not introduced until the reign of Edward IV, and that rapiers were not a medieval weapon.[12] In other words, this argument assumes that the audience, which was radically heterogeneous, had a fairly homogeneous historical consciousness. It assumes that the general populace, that 95 per cent of the population who were not noble,[13] the majority of whom could not read,[14] all had a similar, more than rudimentary historical knowledge: they knew their kings and queens, knew the big facts and dates.

These assumptions seem to have been inferred from the explosion of historical writing and increased historiographic sophistication that marked Elizabeth's reign. Critics such as Irving Ribner begin their studies of the Renaissance English history play by examining the 'new birth of historical writing in England.'[15] Shakespeare's history plays were popular, it is argued, because they were part of the flood of chronicles, chronicle epitomes, popular histories, historical broadsheets, and historical poems that were published in the second half of the sixteenth century. They rode the crest of the increased historical consciousness, as did the *Mirror* itself.

Certainly there was an increase in history reading and writing in this period.[16] As we have seen, the *Mirror* was first published to take advantage of this boom. But to what degree was the general public, the bulk of Shakespeare's audience, most especially the illiterate, caught up in this revolution in historiography? Perhaps not much at all. What did the unlettered, the sailors and apprentices, yeomen and barbers who attended the theatres, know of the very facts of history?[17] Here the evidence is slight. Illiteracy would not necessarily prevent the purchase of broadsheets, which could feature decorative woodblock prints of royalty and family trees.[18] There were many ballads on historical subjects, and they were often censored for their topicality.[19] But those same ballads usually addressed an immediate political crisis. There is no reason to believe that the ballad would still be sung in the same form a generation later, and so it would not necessarily act as a repository of historical fact. Most of the ballads on historical figures were more romanticized fictions – featuring, for example, Good King Hal pretending to be a commoner – than historical records. They offered nothing in the way of information except for the name of the monarch in question. In like fashion, chapbooks tended to use historical figures primarily for their folk appeal.[20] Nor were there, except in some villages in Wales, anything like 'village remembrancers.'[21]

One of the most obvious venues for the transmission of historical fact was through a trickle-down from the literate. Tessa Watt discusses the country recreations of reading aloud among village and parish members.[22] But one might wonder what gentry, no matter how altruistic or wealthy, would lug a folio volume of Holinshed to the alehouse for the education of his honest neighbours. A popular history, like the anecdotal and sententious *Mirror*, would be much more accessible.[23] The more obvious place for the illiterate to receive their history was in the church sermon. But, as Daniel Woolf has argued,

> for most ordinary people, the Creation, the Flood, and the story of Christ were much more familiar historical landmarks than the Norman Conquest or Magna Carta ... In his notes for a homily on rebellion, Archbishop Cranmer, for instance, listed Old Testament examples such as Dathan and Absalom side by side with the architects of more recent 'tumults in England,' Jack Cade and Jack Straw. Even if he regarded all of these names as being equally historical, Cranmer would likely have understood the temporal distance between them. But to an ordinary churchgoer, listening to such examples, the nuances of time and place would be lost, and the illustrative material would blur into a vague and fuzzy but very real past.[24]

This unintentional process of anachronism, combined with oral culture's tendency to 'telescope' past chronology, seems to have resulted in a popular knowledge of the historical past that was selective, riddled with anachronisms and folklore, and often wildly incorrect.[25]

Certainly, the continual comparisons to Richard that plagued Elizabeth I, comparisons that emphasized, at least in the first part of her reign, her dependence on flatterers, would seem to indicate a general knowledge of Richard as dissolute.[26] But Richard does not seem to have made a great impression on popular culture elsewhere; he is not a mainstay of the chapbooks or ballads, as were such heroes as Henry V. The one event of Richard's reign that we might assume lived in the popular historical consciousness, the Peasant's Rebellion, is not mentioned in Shakespeare's play. And the depiction of Richard II in *A Mirror for Magistrates*, which was one of Shakespeare's sources for the play, is crude and reductivist. The King, 'mangled, with blew woundes, lying pale and wanne al naked vpon the cold stones in Paules church' (1: 111) confesses to having being 'ruled all by lust':

I set my minde, to feede, to spoyle, to iust,
Three meales a day could skarce content my mawe,
And all to augment my lecherous minde that must
To Venus pleasures alway be in awe.   (1: 113)

If this was a popular conception of Richard, then Shakespeare's play may be seen as either an education or an antidote. Either way, Keith Thomas is probably correct when he suggests that 'perhaps the over-whelming majority, of popular beliefs about the past had literary origins.'[27]

Indeed, Thomas Nashe's defence of playing in *Pierce Penilesse his Supplication to the Divell* (1592) suggests that the historical material of the history plays was new to a good percentage of the audience: 'First, for the subject of them (for the most part) it is borrowed out of our English chronicles, wherein our forefathers valiant actes (that haue lyne long buried in rustie brasse and worme-eaten bookes) are reuiued, and they themselves raysed from the graue of obliuion, and brought to pleade their aged honours in open presence.'[28] Thomas Heywood, in his *Apology for Actors* (1612), makes the connection between historical drama and audience education even more clear: 'Thirdly, playes have made the ignorant more apprehensive, taught the unlearned the knowledge of many famous histories, instructed such as cannot reade in the discovery of all our English chronicles; and what man have you now of that weake capacity that cannot discourse of any notable thing recorded even from William the Conquerour, nay, from the landing of Brute, untill this day?'[29]

So the factual past to which the represented self of this and other his-tory plays might maintain some continuity may not have existed for a large percentage of the audience outside of the events represented in the play itself. They would not have caught the anachronisms, nor would they have noticed the errors in fact or the compression in histor-ical time that mark *Richard II* and other history plays. The play's celebration of past historical figures such as Edward III and Wood-stock, and the scenes of historical explication, such as 1.2, in which the Duchess of Gloucester reminds John of Gaunt of his own ancestry, may have less to do with the play's celebration of medieval heroism and its depiction of a nascent modern political state under the rule of Bolingbroke than with the practical consideration of constructing a historical past for audience comprehension and character reaction.

As for the shape of history, the citizenry would probably have known it only through popular representations such as the *Mirror* and Shakespeare's plays, and that shape, with a few exceptions, would have been tragic.[30] Nashe defends plays in part by pointing to their dominant narrative: 'they shew the ill successe of treason, the fall of hastie climbers, the wretched ende of vsurpers, the miserie of ciuill dissention, & howe iust God is euermore in punishing of murther.'[31] So, in *Richard II*, Shakespeare does not assume a nascent modern historical consciousness on his audience's part. Rather, he alludes to a historical teleology, to a notion of history's form. Shakespeare does not play to the audience's familiarity with Machiavelli or Bodin, but he assumes their knowledge of *A Mirror for Magistrates*, or at least the *de casibus* form that it epitomized. Behind the allusions to the tragic form in this play, and in the history plays in general, lies, not the classical precedent of Seneca or the pseudo-Aristotelian critical imperatives of the Italian commentators like Castelvetro, but the tragic teleology of history as it was popularized in books like the *Mirror*. To be a tragic hero in the history plays is not to transcend the form, to transcend history, but rather to enter it, to become an object of historical providence.

This explains the initial instability of Richard's character in the play. Richard attempts to construct a historical self in response to changing events, and this results in his writing himself into several roles in the play, to author himself in different ways. He would be a sun king, holding his 'too great a court / And liberal largess' (1.4.43–4), but the solar imagery of the play depicts his eclipse by Bolingbroke. He would be a warrior, but his campaign in Ireland leads to disaster. He would be Christ, but his self-aggrandizement – Christ 'in twelve, / Found truth in all but one; I, in twelve thousand, none' (4.1.170–1) – drives him to out-Christ Christ, and makes the comparison ridiculous. He is successful, ultimately, only in his role as tragic hero.

The process by which Richard finally adopts the tragic narrative as defining his historical self is itself reminiscent of the *de casibus* form to which Richard alludes. In 3.2, Richard arrives back from the wars in Ireland confident in his ability to rid the country of Bolingbroke and the rebels by his mere presence in the realm. He says,

For every man that Bolingbroke hath press'd

To lift shrewd steel against our golden crown,
God for his Richard hath in heavenly pay
A glorious angel   (58–61)

Salisbury enters to tell Richard that the Welsh troops have 'dispers'd and fled' (74), and immediately Richard turns pale. He tells his followers, 'All souls that will be safe, fly from my side / For time hath set a blot upon my pride' (80–1). Bolstered by his supporters, he rallies, only to hear of the death of his supporters Bushy, Greene, and the Earl of Wiltshire. He then calls for the sad stories and draws a *contemptus mundi* moral through the image of 'antic Death' keeping court within 'the hollow crown / That rounds the mortal temples of a king' (160–1). His spirits rise briefly when he is chided by Richmond, but when he learns of the desertion of York he rejects any further attempts to dissuade him from his adopted role, or rather narrative: 'Let no man speak again / To alter this, for counsel is but vain' (213–14). The scene, with it ups and downs, its almost sadistic reversals of fortune, recalls in miniature the form of the *de casibus* collections to which Richard alludes. They, too, present a series of rises and inevitable falls that, when placed together, describe Thomas Browne's 'serpentine and crooked line.'

The next time we see Richard, in the Flint Castle scene (3.3), he rushes towards a tragic end, offering, unbidden, to give 'my large kingdom for a little grave, / A little little grave, an obscure grave' (153–4). His ability to summon up all the possible humiliations that majesty is prone to – 'Must he submit? ... Must he be depos'd? ... Must he lose / The name of king?' (143–6) – also suggests an allusion to the *de casibus* form, with its concatenation of tragedies, rather than the facts of a particular history. In the famous mirror scene, Richard says

        I'll read enough
When I do see the very book indeed
Where all my sins are writ, and that's myself.
    ...
Give me that glass, and therein will I read.   (4.1.273–6)

Richard attempts to equate the image of the physical self with the story of the self. He tries to read his history, the historical self that he has authored, into the mirror image. He fails, for the mirror lies: 'O flatt'ring glass, / Like to my followers in prosperity, / Thou dost beguile me' (279–81). It also fails because the narrative is not finished. The image Richard seeks will be the totality of his life set in the *de casibus* pattern. That cannot be found in 'a flatt'ring glass,' but it can be found in *A Mirror for Magistrates*. This is the mirror of history, in which all rulers may read their fates.

There are two points here. First, Shakespeare has Richard write himself into a popular conception of history. The subject he creates is the object of the *de casibus* history tradition through which his story, or at least the shape of the story, was popularly known. The process is analogous to the famous scene in *Troilus and Cressida* in which Pandarus and the lovers unwittingly project themselves into their Elizabethan reputations. Richard moves to present himself as the *re*presentation that made his historical existence understandable to the audience. Second, Richard writes himself into the history he has read; he is the subject objectifying itself. And, by adding to the story, or, rather, the narrative aggregate that proves the metanarrative of history, Richard is at once rewriting it, by expanding it, and confirming it: his life fits the pattern, and therefore proves the teleology. In Richard's penultimate scene, he bids farewell to his wife by enjoining her to keep his story alive in a *de casibus* aggregate:

> In winter's tedious nights sit by the fire
> With good old folks, and let them tell thee tales
> Of woeful ages long ago betid;
> And ere thou bid good night, to quite their griefs
> Tell thou the lamentable tale of me,
> And send the hearers weeping to their beds   (5.1.40–5)

So, in *Richard II* we have a character who moves from what is, for all intents and purposes, a newly created, dramatic, past towards a popular vision of the form of history, and it is this latter vision that informs the dramatic narrative and audience expectation of historical being. Between the moving from and moving towards lies the tension of the dramatic present and the unstable self. And it is in that tension that Richard experiments with roles, infuriates his followers, and loses audience sympathy. When the movement towards a tragic definition dominates, when Richard decides to become a sad story, he gains dignity and audience sympathy. This is the satisfaction of a foregone conclusion.

All of this emphasizes a disjunction between the history of Shakespeare's plays and popular knowledge. While Shakespeare will play *to* a general knowledge of the form of history, he will play *with* the content of that history, both informing and complicating existing perceptions. This disjunction between the popular perception of history and the historical subject of the drama, between audience knowledge and dramatic representation, finds an image in the portrayal of the common people in *Richard II*. Except for the symbolic garden and groom scenes, the common people are not represented, but we are told about them. We know they do not love the king (2.1.246–7), and they are quick to side with Bolingbroke (3.2.112–20). We do not hear of them doing anything except preparing to fight; for the most part, they are passive. They watch Bolingbroke's ride towards banishment (1.4.23–36) and Richard's ride of disgrace (5.2.23–36). They watch the spectacle of their betters, marvelling at the rise of one and the fall of the other. Similarly, in the *Mirror*, Richard offers this post-mortem lament: 'The Kyng whych erst kept all the realme in doute, / The veryest rascall now dare checke and lowte' (112). Once again the commons – and 'rascal' at this time could mean simply 'a person of the lowest class ... a man of low birth or station' (*Oxford English Dictionary*) – gaze on their betters. They are distanced from the events of history, participating as critics, as an audience.

A similar, though more complex, effect is created by anachronism in those plays of the Henriad that do depict the lower classes. The world of the Boar's Head Tavern, where the patrons drink the sack that had not been popularized yet, is clearly Elizabethan. This is the case, in part, because Shakespeare had no sources for the history of the lower classes; social history had yet to be invented.[32] But it also reflects an unarticulated assumption: history, the broad patterns of events, is something that happens to the great, not the audience watching its representation. Ironically, the great, the Richards, because they are recorded as objects in the teleological plan of history, have the stability to create themselves as historical subjects. For them, the self is formed by the constraints of history: its own self-awareness of history predetermines its fate. The historical subject is trapped by its knowledge of itself as historical object. The lower classes, because they are unrecorded, do not exist as objects, do not exist as subjects. They do not author themselves, but remain unstable: at best an audience, at worst a mob. No mirror reflects their experience of history.

Notes

Introduction

1 See, for example, Willard Farnham, *The Medieval Heritage of Elizabethan Tragedy*, 283–4.
2 See, among others, Howard Baker, *Introduction to Tragedy: A Study in Development of Form in* Gorboduc, The Spanish Tragedy, *and* Titus Andronicus, 204–5; William Peery, 'Tragic Retribution in the 1559 *Mirror for Magistrates*,' 116–30.
3 Lily B. Campbell, ed., *The Mirror for Magistrates*, 51.
4 One exception is Henry Ansgar Kelly, who discusses the *Mirror* as history in his *Divine Providence in the England of Shakespeare's Histories*, 163–82. He makes it very clear, however, that he considered the *Mirror* to be very bad history.
5 See Irving Ribner, *The English History Play in the Age of Shakespeare*, rev. ed., 26.

1: Printing the *Mirror*

1 For an overview of Wayland's life, see H.J. Byrom, 'John Wayland – Printer, Scrivener, and Litigant.'
2 Pynson brought out editions in 1494 and 1527. The earlier edition is available in facsimile: Giovanni Boccaccio, *The Fall of Princys, Princessys and Other Nobles*, The English Experience 777.
3 All references to the text of the *Mirror* are to Lily B. Campbell, ed., *The Mirror for Magistrates* (Cambridge: Cambridge UP, 1938) and *Parts Added to* The Mirror for Magistrates (Cambridge: Cambridge UP, 1946). These titles are referred to parenthetically in the text as vols. 1 and 2, respectively. In accor-

dance with scholarly tradition, and to avoid confusion about prose and poetry passages, page numbers rather than line numbers are given. I have eliminated double capitalizations. All references to Richard Niccols, *A Winter Nights Vision* (London, 1610) are cited as STC 18526.

4 Quoted in Edward Hutton, Introduction, xcvi.

5 For an overview of Boccaccio's sources, see Patricia May Gathercole, *Laurent de Premierfait's* Des Cas des Nobles Hommes et Femmes, 11–15, and Willard Farnham, *The Medieval Heritage of Elizabethan Tragedy*, 75–8.

6 Herbert G. Wright, *Boccaccio in England from Chaucer to Tennyson*, 4.

7 For a full treatment of Premierfait's adaptions of Boccaccio, see Gathercole, *Laurent de Premierfait's* Des Cas des Nobles Hommes et Femmes, especially 18–21.

8 See G.S. Purkis, 'Laurent de Premierfait: First French Translator of the *Decameron*,' 27–8.

9 All citations of *Fall of Princes* are of Henry Bergen's edition: Early English Texts Society, Extra Series, nos. 121–4 (London: Oxford UP, 1924–7), 4 vols. Book and line numbers are given in the text. I have omitted the underlining that Bergen uses to note Old English characters.

10 See Larry Scanlon, *Narrative, Authority, and Power: The Medieval Exemplum and the Chaucerian Tradition*, 329–50, for a discussion of the nationalist politics of translation in Lydgate.

11 For a survey of Lydgate's adaptions of Premierfait, see Gathercole, *Laurent de Premierfait's* Des Cas des Nobles Hommes et Femmes, 33–8, and her article 'Lydgate's *Fall of Princes* and the French Version of Boccaccio's *De Casibus*.' See also Wright, *Boccaccio in England from Chaucer to Tennyson*, 5–22.

12 For a survey of Lydgate's indebtedness to Gloucester, see Eleanor P. Hammond, 'Poet and Patron in the *Fall of Princes*: Lydgate and Humphrey of Gloucester.'

13 For the history of early printing of *Fall of Princes*, see A.S.G. Edwards, 'The Influence of Lydgate's *Fall of Princes* c. 1440–1559: A Survey,' and Henry R. Plomer, *Wynkyn De Worde & His Contemporaries from the Death of Caxton to 1535*, 113–8.

14 See George Cavendish, *Metrical Visions*, 9–11, for Cavendish's indebtedness to Lydgate. For a life of Cavendish, see George Cavendish, *The Life and Death of Cardinal Wolsey*, xiii–xxvi.

15 All references to *Metrical Visions* are to the Edwards edition.

16 See William Jackson, 'Wayland's Edition of *The Mirror for Magistrates*.'

17 See E. Arber, *A Transcript of the Registers of the Company of Stationers of London, 1554–1640*, vol. 1, xxxiii.

18 See F.J. Levy, *Tudor Historical Thought*, 187.

19 H. De Vocht, ed., *Jasper Heywood and his Translations of Seneca's 'Troas,' 'Thyestes' and 'Hercules Furens,'* 102.

20 The best biography of Baldwin is Eveline I. Feasey's 'William Baldwin.

21 This book would get Marshe in some trouble: Cooper objected to this unsanctioned pirating and counted 'almost five hundred fautes and errours eyther of the printer, or els of hym that undertooke the correction.' See H.S. Bennett, *English Books & Readers, 1475 to 1557*, 129–30 and 238.

22 Lily B. Campbell, 'Humphrey Duke of Gloucester & Elianor Cobham His Wife in *A Mirror for Magistrates*,' in *Collected Papers*, 209.

23 The only overview of the life and works of Niccols is in *Selected Poems*, ed. Glyn Pursglove.

24 Sir Philip Sidney, *The Prose Works*, vol. 3, 37.

25 For a brief overview of *Mirror* spin-offs, see Louis R. Zocca, *Elizabethan Narrative Poetry*, 36ff.

2: History

1 Lily B. Campbell, 'Tudor Conceptions of History and Tragedy in *A Mirror for Magistrates*,' in *Collected Papers*, 284–6.

2 See Achsah Guibbory, *The Map of Time: Seventeenth-Century English Literature and Ideas of Pattern in History*, 8–18, and Herschel Baker, *The Race of Time: Three Lectures on Renaissance Historiography*, 59–63.

3 See Anne Higgins, 'Medieval Notions of the Structure of Time,' especially 232–8.

4 C.A. Patrides, *The Grand Design of God*, 7.

5 See St Augustine, *The City of God*, especially XII, 13.

6 Patrides, *Grand Design of God*, 48. See also Frank E. Manuel, *Shapes of Philosophical History*, 1–69.

7 See Antonia Gransden, *Historical Writing in England*, vol. 2, 454–9.

8 See Higgins, 'Medieval Notions,' 235–6.

9 Patrides, *Grand Design of God*, 18–21. See also Higgins, 'Medieval Notions,' 238–47.

10 Guibbory, *Map of Time*, 1.

11 See Richard Helgerson, *Forms of Nationhood: The Elizabethan Writing of England*, 11–12.

12 Henry Ansgar Kelly, *Ideas and Forms of Tragedy from Aristotle to the Middle Ages*, xiv.

13 For a polemical discussion of this tradition, see the introduction to Jonathan Dollimore's second edition of *Radical Tragedy: Religion, Ideology and Power in the Drama of Shakespeare and his Contemporaries*, especially xvi–xx.

14 Kelly, *Ideas and Forms of Tragedy*, xv.

15 Giovanni Boccaccio, *The Fates of Illustrious Men*, 1–2.

16 Kelly makes this argument at length in *Ideas and Forms of Tragedy*. He summarizes it in *Chaucerian Tragedy*, 4ff.

17 Larry Scanlon, 'The King's Two Voices: Narrative and Power in Hoccleve's *Regement of Princes*,' 242.

18 J.A. Burrow, *Ricardian Poetry: Chaucer, Gower, Langland and the* Gawain *Poet*, 83.

19 Guibbory, *Map of Time*, 6.

20 Allan H. Gilbert, *Machiavelli's* Prince *and Its Forerunners*, 4.

21 John of Salisbury, *Policratus: Of the Frivolities of Courtiers and the Footprints of Philosophers*, xxii.

22 See Hoccleve, *Works*, vol. 3.

23 See Joseph Haslewood, ed., *The Mirror for Magistrates*, 2 vols.

24 Sir Philip Sidney, *The Prose Works*, vol. 3, 14.

25 See ibid., 37.

26 F.J. Levy, *Tudor Historical Thought*, 13–14. See also Donald R. Kelley, 'The Theory of History,' 748–50.

27 Louis B. Wright, *Middle-Class Culture in Elizabethan England*, 297–8.

28 See Ernst Breisach, *Historiography: Ancient, Medieval, & Modern*, 2d ed., 173–7.

29 F. Smith Fussner, *The Historical Revolution: English Historical Writing and Thought, 1580–1640*, 193.

30 Daniel Woolf, *The Idea of History in Early Stuart England: Erudition, Ideology, and 'The Light of Truth' from the Accession of James I to the Civil War*, 143.

31 J.B. Bury, *The Idea of Progress: An Inquiry into Its Origin and Growth*, 43. For the political impetus of this shift, see Felix Gilbert, *Machiavelli and Guicciardini*, 128ff. For a discussion of early signs of this shift in humanist historians, see Gransden, *Historical Writing*, 427.

32 Levy, *Tudor Historical Thought*, 237.

33 John Guy, *Tudor England*, 415. For an overview of the influence of Tacitus, see Kenneth C. Schellhase, *Tacitus in Renaissance Political Thought*, especially 157–66. Daniel Woolf reminds us that this was not a clear schematic division, but rather an attitudinal position of historians to the past: *The Idea of History*, 11.

34 Ivo Kamps, *Historiography and Ideology in Stuart Drama*, 31.

35 See Eveline Iris Feasey, 'The Licensing of the *Mirror for Magistrates*,' 182.

36 See Annabel Patterson, *Reading* Hollinshed's Chronicles, 154–61. for a summary of the Throckmorton case and its relation to the *Mirror*.

37 Lily B. Campbell, 'Tudor Conceptions of History and Tragedy in *A Mirror for Magistrates*,' in *Collected Papers*, 300.

38 Herbert G. Wright notes that 'the advice given to the student of "English politicks", in a fifteenth-century manuscript that belonged to the earl of Leicester, [was] to read "Seneck and John Bocasse"': *Boccaccio in England from Chaucer to Tennyson*, 3.

39 Law, Scanlon, *Narrative, Authority, and Power: The Medieval Exemplum and the Chaucerian Tradition*, 134.

40 Herbert Grabes, *The Mutable Glass: Mirror-Imagery in Titles and Texts of the Middle Ages and English Renaissance*, 23ff. Grabes discusses the *Mirror* in the context of *de contemptu mundi* literature (89–90) and 'Mirrors of human vanity and polemical writings' (58) but concludes that the book does not fit in either category comfortably.

41 See Louis R. Zocca, *Elizabethan Narrative Poetry*, 23.

42 For a recent example of this tendency, see Richard Hillman, *Self-Speaking in Medieval and Early Modern Drama: Subjectivity, Discourse and the Stage*, 78.

43 This is the central argument of Helgerson's book. See also Claire McEachern, *The Poetics of English Nationhood, 1590–1612*.

44 For a discussion of Tudor bureaucratic corruption, see Joel Hurstfield, *Freedom, Corruption and Government in Elizabethan England*, especially 137ff.

45 For a history of *The Brut*, see Charles L. Kingsford, *English Historical Literature in the Fifteenth Century*, 113–39.

46 T.D. Kendrick, *British Antiquity*, 2.

47 Edmund Spenser, *The Prose Works*, 86.

48 See Arthur B. Ferguson, *Utter Antiquity: Perceptions of Prehistory in Renaissance England*, 47.

49 See ibid., 62ff.

50 Scanlon, *Narrative, Authority, and Power*, 35.

51 For a discussion of Higgins's use of classical history in the *Mirror*, see Douglas Bush, 'Classical Lives in *The Mirror for Magistrates*.'

52 See Guibbory, *Map of Time*, 3–4.

53 See Joseph M. Levine, *Humanism and History: Origins of Modern English Historiography*, 41–5.

54 Roberta F. Brinkley, *Arthurian Legend in the Seventeenth Century*, 9–17.

55 Ibid., 63.

56 See Woolf, *The Idea of History*, 63.

57 A.W. Ward, and A.R. Waller, *The Cambridge History of English Literature*, vol. 3, 197.

58 Quoted in Philip Corrigan and Derek Sayer, *The Great Arch: English State Formation as Cultural Revolution*, 55.

59 Frank Freeman Foster, *The Politics of Stability: A Portrait of the Rulers in Elizabethan London*, 13.

60 See A.J. Fletcher, 'Honour, Reputation and Local Officeholding in Elizabethan and Stuart England.' Also see Woolf, *The Idea of History*, 12.
61 Frank Whigham, *Ambition and Privilege: The Social Tropes of Elizabethan Courtesy Theory*, 2.
62 Ibid., 32.
63 See Diane Bornstein, *Mirrors of Courtesy*, 124–5, for a discussion of this tradition in courtesy literature.
64 History has been much less kind to Leighton. See Campbell, ed., *Parts Added*, 371.
65 See Franklin B. Williams Jr, *Index of Dedications and Commendatory Verses in English Books before 1641*, 99.
66 Part of Woolf's definition of antiquarian discourse is helpful here: 'they were devoid of moral or exemplary content; ... their authors were almost entirely unconcerned with the rhetorical conventions of form which applied to true history-writing': *The Idea of History*, 18.
67 See H.S. Bennett, *Beware the Cat*, 10–12, or STC 1245, sig. A3–A5.
68 Donald A. Stauffer, *English Biography before 1700*, is wrong when he says the dream convention 'is followed without deviation into the seventeenth century' (52). While dreams do play a part in the Baldwin editions of the *Mirror*, they do not frame the entire work.
69 Henry Ansgar Kelly's criticism of the Baldwin editions of the *Mirror* as being 'inconsistent' in their treatment of English history is then, I would argue, misplaced. The acknowledgment of the impossibility of absolute historical coherence is exactly what made those editions historigraphically significant. See Kelly, *Divine Providence in the England of Shakespeare's Histories*, 165.
70 See Peter Burke, *The Fortunes of the Courtier: The European Reception of Castiglione's* Cortegiano, 19–21.
71 Whigham, *Ambition and Privilege*, 28.
72 There is at least one direct link between courtesy literature and the *Mirror*: Thomas Sackville wrote a sonnet for the introduction to Hoby's English translation of *The Courtier*.
73 Wright, *Boccaccio in England*, 330.
74 David Cressy, *Literacy and Social Order: Reading and Writing in Tudor and Stuart England*, 8.
75 Ward and Waller, *Cambridge History of English Literature*, 198.

3: Tragedy and Fortune

1 William C. Strange, '*The Monk's Tale*: A Generous View,' 167.
2 An example of this tendency can be found in Donald V. Stump's 'Sidney's

Concept of Tragedy in the *Apology* and in the *Arcadia*,' 60. Stump's condemnation of the *Mirror* is clearly based on a contrast with Greek tragic models.

3 Willard Farnham, *The Medieval Heritage of Elizabethan Tragedy* 151; Madeleine Doran, *Endeavors of Art: A Study of Form in Elizabethan Drama*, 120.

4 Part of what Lydgate says, however, is bluff: he never actually read Seneca. See Henry Ansgar Kelly, *Ideas and Forms of Tragedy from Aristotle to the Middle Ages*, 170.

5 All references to Lydgate's *Troy Book* cite Henry Bergen's two-volume edition, Early English Text Society, extra ser. 97, 103, 106 (London: Kegan Paul, Trench, Trübner, 1906; rpt. Millwood, NY: Kraus, 1975). Book and line numbers are cited in the text. I have modernized Old English characters.

6 See Larry Scanlon, *Narrative, Authority, and Power: The medieval exemplum and the Chaucerian tradition*, 219.

7 See M.C. Seymour, 'Chaucer's Early Poem *De Casibus Virorum Illustrium*.'

8 See Edward M. Socola, 'Chaucer's Development of Fortune in the "Monk's Tale,"' 160–1.

9 All references to Chaucer are to Larry D. Benson, ed., *The Riverside Chaucer* (Boston: Houghton Mifflin, 1987).

10 D.W. Robertson, Jr, 'Chaucerian Tragedy,' 86.

11 Monica E. McAlpine, *The Genre of* Troilus and Criseyde, 20–1.

12 See Henry Ansgar Kelly's argument in *Chaucerian Tragedy*, 51–4.

13 Robertson, Jr, 'Chaucerian Tragedy,' 87.

14 Socola, 'Chaucer's Development of Fortune,' 160.

15 See ibid., 165 and 167.

16 Strange, 'The *Monk's Tale*,' 171.

17 Johan Ramazani, 'Chaucer's Monk: The Poetics of Abbreviation, Aggression, and Tragedy,' 261.

18 Joella Owen Brown, 'Chaucer's Daun Piers: One Monk or Two?' 49.

19 Kelly, *Ideas and Forms of Tragedy*, 221.

20 Robertson, Jr, 'Chaucerian Tragedy,' 87.

21 Howard R. Patch, *The Goddess Fortuna in Medieval Literature*, 17–19.

22 See D.R. Woolf, *The Idea of History in Early Stuart England: Erudition, Ideology, and 'The Light of Truth' from the Accession of James I to the Civil War*, 7–8.

23 Scanlon, *Narrative, Authority, and Power*, 122.

24 The trope of the winter landscape that Sackville popularized, though did not invent, would start a vogue for melancholy winter poems. See Alan T. Bradford, 'Mirrors of Mutability: Winter Landscapes in Tudor Poetry.'

25 For a discussion of Sackville's use of Vergil, see Jeannine Bohlmeyer, 'Mythology in Sackville's "Induction" and "Complaint."'

26 See Normand Berlin, *Thomas Sackville*, 36–7, for a discussion of the Chaucer reference.

27 See, for example, William Peery, 'Tragic Retribution in the 1559 *Mirror for Magistrates*'; Frederick Kiefer, 'Fortune and Providence in the *Mirror for Magistrates*.'
28 Herschel Baker, *The Race of Time: Three Lectures on Renaissance Historiography*, 64.
29 Sir Thomas Brown, *Religio Medici*, in *'Religio Medici' and Other Works*, 17.

4: Women

1 Among the many important works on the subject of literary representations of Renaissance women must be figured Francis Utley's *The Crooked Rib*; Louis B. Wright's 'The Popular Controversy over Women,' in *Middle-Class Culture in Elizabethan England*; Gamaliel Bradford's *Elizabethan Women*; Suzanne Hull's *Chaste, Silent & Obedient*; Linda Woodbridge's *Women and the English Renaissance*.
2 See Constance Jordan, *Renaissance Feminism: Literary Texts and Political Models*, 35–40; see also Jordan's 'Boccaccio's In-Famous Women: Gender and Civic Virtue in the *De mulieribus claris*,' 25–45; Woodbridge, *Women and the English Renaissance*, 14–15.
3 See, for example, Heather Dubrow, 'A Mirror for Complaints: Shakespeare's *Lucrece* and Generic Tradition,' 400.
4 Jordan, *Renaissance Feminism*, 35–40.
5 Herbert G. Wright, *Boccaccio in England from Chaucer to Tennyson*, 28–9.
6 For a discussion of the Morley text, see Herbert G. Wright, Introduction in Henry Parker, Lord Morley, *Forty-Six Lives Translated from Boccaccio's De Claris Mulieribus*, lxix–lxxi.
7 Jordan, 'Boccaccio's In-Famous Women,' 25.
8 Woodbridge, *Women and the English Renaissance*, 16–17.
9 Janis Butler Holm, 'The Myth of Feminist Humanism: Thomas Salter's *The Mirrhor of Modestie*,' 211.
10 Dubrow suggests that *A Mirror for Magistrates* itself evolved towards greater gender equality: 'most obviously, the later volumes include women among their speakers': 'A Mirror for Complaints,' 400. In fact, the excising of the tragedy of Elianor Cobham from the 1559 edition had little to do with gender, and the very next edition of the *Mirror* contained the 'Shore's Wife' tragedy.
11 For an overview of treatments of the Shore legend, see Robert Birley, 'Jane Shore in Literature,' and 'Jane Shore: Some Further Appearances'; James L. Harner, '"The Wofull Lamentation of Mistris Jane Shore": The Popularity of an Elizabethan Ballad.'

12 See Barbara Brown, 'Sir Thomas More and Thomas Churchyard's *Shore's Wife*' for a discussion of Churchyard's indebtedness to More.

13 See Annabel Patterson, *Reading Holinshed's* Chronicles, 217–21, for a discussion of Holinshed's recounting of the Shore story.

14 All references to More are to *Complete Works*, 2 vols., ed. Richard S. Sylvester (New Haven and London: Yale UP, 1963).

15 See Esther Yael Beith-Halahmi, *Angell Faire or Strumpet Lewd: Jane Shore and an Example of Erring Beauty in the 16th Century*, 1:68–9.

16 It is ironic that Humphrey should be excluded from early editions of the *Mirror*, given his role as patron of the *Fall of Princes*. See Eleanor P. Hammond, 'Poet and Patron in the *Fall of Princes*: Lydgate and Humphrey of Gloucester.'

17 I have traced this evolution of the *Mirror* and its relation to late Tudor and early Stuart historiography in 'The *Mirror for Magistrates* and the Politics of Readership.'

18 For a brief overview of other 'mirrors' that imitated *A Mirror for Magistrates*, see Louis R. Zocca, *Elizabethan Narrative Poetry*, 36–46.

19 All references to Daniel are to *The Works*, vol. 1, ed. Alexander B. Grosart (New York: Russell & Russell, 1963).

20 See Beith-Halahmi, *Angell Faire*, 111.

21 All references to Chute are to *Beawtie dishonoured, written vnder the title of Shores wife* (London, 1593), STC 5262.

22 Beith-Halahmi, *Angell Faire*, 128–9.

23 Cites *Churchyards Challenge* (London, 1593), STC 5220.

24 Ronald Primeau, 'Daniel and the *Mirror* Tradition: Dramatic Irony in *The Complaint of Rosamond*,' argues for Daniel's sophisticated and ironic use of the *Mirror* form.

25 All references to Drayton are to *The Works*, vol. 1, ed. J. William Hebel (Oxford: Blackwell, 1961).

26 See Beith-Halahmi, *Angell Faire*, 85.

27 See Utley, *The Crooked Rib*, 51.

28 See Retha M. Warnicke, 'Eulogies for Women: Public Testimony of Their Godly Example and Leadership,' 170.

5: Drama

1 See Sir Philip Sidney, *The Prose Works*, vol. 3, 37.

2 Michael D. Bristol, *Carnival and Theater: Plebian Culture and the Structure of Authority in Renaissance England*, 122–3.

3 Geoffrey Bullough, ed., *Narrative and Dramatic Sources of Shakespeare*, vol. 3, viii.

4 Alexander Leggatt, *Shakespeare's Political Drama: The History Plays and the Roman Plays*, 1.

5 All references to the works of Shakespeare, other than to *King Richard II*, are to *The Complete Works*, 4th ed., ed. David Bevington (New York: HarperCollins, 1992).

6 Shakespeare, *The Complete Works*, 539.

7 Phyllis Rackin, *Stages of History: Shakespeare's English Chronicles*, 25.

8 This is one of the major topics of Annabel Patterson's *Reading Holinshed's Chronicles*.

9 All references to the play are to *King Richard II*, ed. Peter Ure (London: Methuen, 1961).

10 See, for example, Willard Farnham, *The Medieval Heritage of Elizabethan Tragedy*, 416–17. Farnham draws the parallel between Richard's career and the shape of *de casibus* tragedy as epitomized by *A Mirror for Magistrates*, but he sees the 'sad stories' as part of another medieval tradition, the Dance of Death.

11 Marshall Grossman, *'Authors to Themselves': Milton and the Revelation of History*, viii.

12 For example, see Phyllis Rackin's sophisticated argument on anachronism in the history plays: *Stages of History*, 86–145.

13 Peter Laslett, *The World We Have Lost*, 27.

14 On the question of literacy rates, see both David Cressy, *Literacy and the Social Order: Reading and Writing in Tudor and Stuart England*, and Margaret Spufford, *Small Books and Pleasant Histories*, ch. 2.

15 Irving Ribner, *The English History Play in the Age of Shakespeare*, 2.

16 The *Mirror* first made it to the book stalls in 1559, at the beginning of the decade that would see more history books produced than any other period of Elizabeth's reign: H.S. Bennett, *English Books & Readers, 1558 to 1603*, 215.

17 See Andrew Gurr's list of playgoers in *Playgoing in Shakespeare's London*, 191–204.

18 See plate 10, p. 144, in Tessa Watt's *Cheap Print and Popular Piety, 1550–1640* for an example.

19 See Hyder F. Rollins, *Old English Ballads, 1553–1625*, x–xvii, for an account of attempts to suppress ballads during the reigns of Henry VIII, Mary I, and Elizabeth.

20 See Spufford, *Small Books*, 222–4. For a discussion of the historicity of both ballads and chapbooks, see Daniel Woolf, 'Of Danes and Giants: Popular Beliefs about the Past in Early Modern Europe,' 181–2.

21 Daniel Woolf, 'The "Common Voice": History, Folklore and Oral Tradition in Early Modern England,' 37.

22 Watt, *Cheap Print*, 258.

23 Baldwin tells us that the collective of writers who created the early editions of the *Mirror* read the individual tragedies aloud to each other for their opinions: Campbell, ed., *Mirror*, 101 *passim*.

24 Woolf, 'Of Danes and Giants,' 176–7.

25 Woolf, 'Common Voices,' 31.

26 For the comparisons between Richard and Elizabeth, see Lily B. Campbell, *Shakespeare's Histories: Mirrors of Elizabethan Policy*, 173ff.

27 Keith Thomas, *The Perception of the Past in Early Modern England*, 7

28 Reprinted in *Shakespeare Society of London Publications*, vol. 9 (Nendeln, Liechtenstein: Kraus, 1966), 59–60.

29 Reprinted in *Shakespeare Society of London Publications*, vol. 6 (Nendeln, Liechtenstein: Kraus, 1966), 52–3.

30 When Elizabethan dramatists looked for tragic subject matter, they turned so repeatedly to history that critics such as Irving Ribner have declared that it is impossible to distinguish the history play from tragedy as dramatic genres: Ribner, *The English History Play in the Age of Shakespeare*, 26.

31 *Shakespeare Society of London*, vol. 9, 61.

32 See Arthur B. Ferguson, *Clio Unbound*, ch. 1.

Bibliography

Arber, E. *A Transcript of the Registers of the Company of Stationers of London, 1554–1640*. 5 vols. London, 1875.

Augustine, St. *The City of God*. Trans. Marcus Dods. New York: Random House, 1950.

Baker, Herschel. *The Race of Time: Three Lectures on Renaissance Historiography*. Toronto: U of Toronto P, 1967.

Baker, Howard. *Introduction to Tragedy: A Study in Development of Form in Gorboduc, The Spanish Tragedy, and Titus Andronicus*. New York: Russell & Russell, 1965.

Baldwin, William. *Beware the Cat*. London, 1584 [STC 1245].

Beith-Halahmi, Esther Yael. *Angell Faire or Strumpet Lewd: Jane Shore and an Example of Erring Beauty in the 16th Century*. Elizabethan & Renaissance Studies 26. 2 vols. Salzburg: Institut fur Englische Sprache und Literatur, 1974.

Bennett, H.S. *English Books & Readers, 1475 to 1557*. Cambridge: Cambridge UP, 1952.

– *English Books & Readers, 1558 to 1603*. Cambridge: Cambridge UP, 1985.

Benson, Larry D., ed. *The Riverside Chaucer*. 3d ed. Boston: Houghton Mifflin, 1987.

Berlin, Normand. *Thomas Sackville*. New York: Twayne, 1974.

Birley, Robert. 'Jane Shore in Literature.' *Etoniana* 125–6 (1972): 391–407.

– 'Jane Shore: Some Further Appearances.' *Etoniana* 128 (1973): 448–57.

Blundeville, Thomas. *The true order and Methode of wryting and reading Hystories*. The English Experience 908. London, 1574; Amsterdam: Theatrum Orbis Terrarrum; Norwood, NJ: Walter. J. Johnson, 1976.

Boccaccio, Giovanni. *The Fall of Princys, Princessys and Other Nobles*. The English Experience 777. London, 1494; Amsterdam: Theatrum Orbis Terrarrum, 1976.

– *The Fates of Illustrious Men.* Trans. Louis Brewer Hall. New York: Frederick Ungar, 1965.

Bohlmeyer, Jeannine. 'Mythology in Sackville's "Induction" and "Complaint."' *Costerus* 1 (1972): 9–23.

Bornstein, Diane. *Mirrors of Courtesy.* Hamden, CT: Archon, 1975.

Bradford, Alan T. 'Mirrors of Mutability: Winter Landscapes in Tudor Poetry.' *English Literary Renaissance* (1974): 3–39.

Bradford, Gamaliel. *Elizabethan Women.* Boston: Houghton Mifflin, 1977.

Breisach, Ernst. *Historiography: Ancient, Medieval, & Modern.* 2nd ed. Chicago and London: Chicago UP, 1994.

Brinkley, Roberta F. *Arthurian Legend in the Seventeenth Century.* New York: Octagon, 1967.

Bristol, Michael D. *Carnival and Theater: Plebeian Culture and the Structure of Authority in Renaissance England.* New York and London: Methuen, 1985.

Brown, Barbara. 'Sir Thomas More and Thomas Churchyard's *Shore's Wife.*' *Yearbook of English Studies* 2 (1972): 41–8.

Brown, Joella Owens. 'Chaucer's Daun Piers: One Monk or Two?' *Criticism* 6 (1964): 44–52.

Browne, Sir Thomas. *'Religio Medici' and Other Works.* Ed. L.C. Martin. Oxford: Oxford UP, 1964.

Budra, Paul. 'The *Mirror for Magistrates* and the Politics of Readership,' *Studies in English Literature, 1500–1900* 32 (1992): 1–13.

Bullough, Geoffrey, ed. *Narrative and Dramatic Sources of Shakespeare,* vol. 3. London: Routledge and Kegan Paul; New York: Columbia UP, 1960.

Burke, Peter. *The Fortunes of the Courtier: The European Reception of Castiglione's* Cortegiano. Cambridge: Polity, 1995.

Burrow, J.A. *Ricardian Poetry: Chaucer, Gower, Langland and the* Gawain *Poet.* London: Routledge & Kegan Paul, 1971.

Bury, J.B. *The Idea of Progress: An Inquiry into Its Origin and Growth.* London: Macmillan, 1920.

Bush, Douglas. 'Classical Lives in *The Mirror for Magistrates.*' *Studies in Philology* 22 (1925): 256–66.

Byrom, H.J. 'John Wayland – Printer, Scrivener, and Litigant.' *The Library* 4th ser., 11 (1931): 312–49.

Campbell, Lily B. *Collected Papers of Lily B. Campbell.* New York: Russell & Russell, 1968.

– ed. *The Mirror for Magistrates.* Cambridge: Cambridge UP, 1938.

– ed. *Parts Added to* The Mirror for Magistrates. Cambridge: Cambridge UP, 1946

– *Shakespeare's Histories: Mirrors of Elizabethan Policy.* San Marino, CA: Huntington, 1963.

Cavendish, George. *The Life and Death of Cardinal Wolsey*. Ed. Richard S. Sylvester. Early English Text Society 243. London: Oxford UP, 1959.

– *Metrical Visions*. Ed. A.S.G. Edwards. Columbia: U of South Carolina P, 1980.

Chute, Anthony. *Beawtie dishonoured, written vnder the title of Shores wife*. London, 1593 [STC 5262].

Churchyard, Thomas. *Churchyard's Challenge*. London, 1593 [STC 5262].

Corrigan, Philip, and Derek Sayer. *The Great Arch: English State Formation as Cultural Revolution*. Oxford: Blackwell, 1985.

Cressy, David. *Literacy and Social Order: Reading and Writing in Tudor and Stuart England*. Cambridge: Cambridge UP, 1980.

Daniel, Samuel. *The Works*, vol. 1. Ed. Alexander B. Grosart. New York: Russell & Russell, 1963.

De Vocht, H., ed. *Jasper Heywood and His Translations of Seneca's 'Troas,' 'Thyestes' and 'Hercules Furens.'* Louvain: A. Uystpruyst, 1913.

Dollimore, Jonathan. *Radical Tragedy: Religion, Ideology and Power in the Drama of Shakespeare and his Contemporaries*. 2d ed. Durham, NC: Duke UP, 1993.

Doran, Madeleine. *Endeavors of Art: A Study of Form in Elizabethan Drama*. Madison: U of Wisconsin P, 1964.

Drayton, Michael. *The Works*, vol. 1. Ed. J. William Hebel. Oxford: Blackwell, 1961.

Dubrow, Heather. 'A Mirror for Complaints: Shakespeare's Lucrece and Generic Tradition.' In *Renaissance Genres: Essays on Theory, History, and Interpretation*. Ed. Barbara Lewalski. Cambridge, MA, and London: Harvard UP, 1986. 399–417.

Edwards, A.S.G. 'The Influence of Lydgate's *Fall of Princes* c. 1440–1559: A Survey.' *Medieval Studies* 39 (1977): 424–39.

Farnham, Willard. *The Medieval Heritage of Elizabethan Tragedy*. New York: Barnes & Noble, 1963.

Feasey, Eveline Iris. 'The Licensing of the *Mirror for Magistrates.*' *The Library* 4th ser., 3 (1922): 177–93.

– 'William Baldwin,' *Modern Language Review* 20.4 (October 1925): 407–18.

Ferguson, Arthur B. *Clio Unbound*. Durham, NC: Duke UP, 1979.

– *Utter Antiquity: Perceptions of Prehistory in Renaissance England*. Durham, NC, and London: Duke UP, 1993.

Fletcher, A.J. 'Honour, Reputation and Local Officeholding in Elizabethan and Stuart England.' In *Order and Disorder in Early Modern England*. Ed. Anthony Fletcher and John Stevenson. Cambridge: Cambridge UP, 1985. 92–115.

Foster, Frank Freeman. *The Politics of Stability: A Portrait of the Rulers in Elizabethan London*. London: Royal Historical Society, 1977.

Fussner, F. Smith. *The Historical Revolution: English Historical Writing and*

Thought, 1580–1640. New York: Columbia UP; London: Routledge and Kegan Paul, 1962.

Gathercole, Patricia May. *Laurent de Premierfait's Des Cas des Nobles Hommes et Femmes*, Studies in Romance Languages and Literatures 74. Chapel Hill: U of North Carolina P, 1968.

– 'Lydgate's *Fall of Princes* and the French Version of Boccaccio's *De Casibus*.' In *Miscellanea Di Studi E Ricerche Sul Quattrocento Francese*. Ed. Franco Simone. Torino: Giappichelli, 1967. 167–78.

Gilbert, Allan H. *Machiavelli's* Prince *and Its Forerunners*. New York: Barnes & Noble, 1938.

Gilbert, Felix. *Machiavelli and Guicciardini*. Princeton, NJ: Princeton UP, 1965.

Grabes, Herbert. *The Mutable Glass: Mirror-Imagery in Titles and Texts of the Middle Ages and English Renaissance*. Trans. Gordon Collier. Cambridge: Cambridge UP, 1982.

Gransden, Antonia. *Historical Writing in England*, vol. 2. London and Henley: Routledge and Kegan Paul, 1982.

Grossman, Marshall. *'Authors to Themselves': Milton and the Revelation of History*. Cambridge: Cambridge UP, 1987.

Guibbory, Achsah. *The Map of Time: Seventeenth-Century English Literature and Ideas of Pattern in History*. Urbana and Chicago: U of Illinois P, 1986.

Gurr, Andrew. *Playgoing in Shakespeare's London*. Cambridge: Cambridge UP, 1987.

Guy, John. *Tudor England*. Oxford: Oxford UP, 1988.

Hammond, Eleanor P. 'Poet and Patron in the *Fall of Princes*: Lydgate and Humphrey of Gloucester.' *Anglia* 38 (1914): 121–36.

Harner, James L. '"The Wofull Lamentation of Mistris Jane Shore": The Popularity of an Elizabethan Ballad.' *Papers of the Bibliographical Society of America* 71 (1977): 137–49.

Haslewood, Joseph, ed. *The Mirror for Magistrates*. 2 vols. London: Lackington, Allen; Longman, Hurst, Rees, and Browne, 1815.

Helgerson, Richard. *Forms of Nationhood: The Elizabethan Writing of England*. Chicago and London: U of Chicago P, 1992.

Heywood, Thomas. *Apology for Actors* (1612). Rpr. in *Shakespeare Society of London Publications*, vol. 6, no. 3. Nendeln, Liechtenstein: Kraus, 1966.

Higgins, Anne. 'Medieval Notions of the Structure of Time,' *Journal of Medieval and Renaissance Studies* 19 (1989): 227–50.

Hillman, Richard. *Self-Speaking in Medieval and Early Modern Drama: Subjectivity, Discourse and the Stage*. New York: St Martin's, 1997.

Hoccleve. *Works*, vol. 3. Ed. Frederick J. Furnivall. Early English Text Society, extra ser. 72. London, 1897.

Holm, Janis Butler. 'The Myth of Feminist Humanism: Thomas Salter's *The Mirrhor of Modestie.*' In *Ambiguous Realities: Women in the Middle Ages and Renaissance.* Ed. Carole Levin and Heanie Watson. Detroit, MI: Wayne State UP, 1987. 197–218.

Hull, Suzanne. *Chaste, Silent & Obedient.* San Marino, CA: Huntington, 1982.

Hurstfield, Joel. *Freedom, Corruption and Government in Elizabethan England.* London: Jonathan Cape, 1973.

Hutton, Edward. Introduction. In Giovanni Boccaccio, *The Decameron,* vol. 1. London: David Nutt, 1909.

Jackson, William. 'Wayland's Edition of *The Mirror for Magistrates.*' *The Library,* 4th ser., 13 (1932–3): 155–7.

John of Salisbury. *Policratus: Of the Frivolities of Courtiers and the Footprints of Philosophers.* Ed. Cary J. Nederman. Cambridge: Cambridge UP, 1990.

Jordan, Constance. 'Boccaccio's In-Famous Women: Gender and Civic Virtue in the *De mulieribus claris.*' In *Ambiguous Realities: Women in the Middle Ages and Renaissance.* Ed. Carole Levin and Heanie Watson. Detroit, MI: Wayne State UP, 1987. 25–47.

– *Renaissance Feminism: Literary Texts and Political Models.* Ithaca, NY, and London: Cornell UP, 1990.

Kamps, Ivo. *Historiography and Ideology in Stuart Drama.* Cambridge: Cambridge UP, 1996.

Kelley, Donald R. 'The Theory of History.' In *The Cambridge History of Renaissance Philosophy.* Gen. ed. Charles B. Schmitt. Cambridge: Cambridge UP, 1988. 746–61.

Kelly, Henry Ansgar. *Chaucerian Tragedy.* Chaucer Studies XXIV. Cambridge: D.S. Brewer, 1997.

– *Divine Providence in the England of Shakespeare's Histories.* Cambridge, MA: Harvard UP, 1970.

– *Ideas and Forms of Tragedy from Aristotle to the Middle Ages.* Cambridge Studies in Medieval Literature 18. Cambridge: Cambridge UP, 1993.

Kendrick, T.D. *British Antiquity.* London: Methuen, 1950.

Kiefer, Frederick. 'Fortune and Providence in the *Mirror for Magistrates.*' *Studies in Philology* 74 (1977): 146–64.

Kingsford, Charles L. *English Historical Literature in the Fifteenth Century.* Oxford: Clarendon, 1913.

Laslett, Peter. *The World We Have Lost,* 2d ed. New York: Scribner's, 1971.

Leggatt, Alexander. *Shakespeare's Political Drama: The History Plays and the Roman Plays.* London and New York: Routledge, 1988.

Levin, Carole, and Jeanie Watson, eds. *Ambiguous Realities: Women in the Middle Ages and Renaissance.* Detroit, MI: Wayne State UP, 1987.

Levine, Joseph M. *Humanism and History: Origins of Modern English Historiography*. Ithaca, NY, and London: Cornell UP, 1987.

Levy, F.J. *Tudor Historical Thought*. San Marino, CA: Huntington, 1967.

Lydgate, John. *Fall of Princes*. Ed. Henry Bergen. 4 vols. Early English Texts Society, Extra Series, nos. 121–4. London: Oxford UP, 1924–7.

– *Troy Book*. Ed. Henry Bergen. 2 vols. Early English Texts Society, Extra Series, nos. 97, 103, 106. London: Kegan Paul, Trench, Trübner, 1906; rpt. Millwood, NY: Kraus, 1975.

Manuel, Frank E. *Shapes of Philosophical History*. London: Allen & Unwin, 1965.

McAlpine, Moncia E. *The Genre of* Troilus and Criseyde. Ithaca, NY, and London: Cornell UP, 1978.

McEachern, Claire. *The Poetics of English Nationhood, 1590–1612*. Cambridge Studies in Renaissance Literature and Culture 13. Cambridge: Cambridge UP, 1996.

More, Thomas. *Complete Works*. Vol. 2. Ed. Richard S. Sylvester. New Haven, CT, and London: Yale UP, 1963.

Nashe, Thomas. *Pierce Penilesse his Supplication to the Divell* (1592). Rpr. in *Shakespeare Society of London*, vol. 9. Nendeln, Liechtenstein: Kraus, 1966.

Niccols, Richard. *Selected Poems*. Ed. Glyn Pursglove. Elizabethan and Renaissance Studies 111. Austria: Institut Für Anglistik und Amerikanistik; Lewiston, NY: Edwin Mellen, 1992.

– *A Winter Nights Vision*. London, 1610 [STC 18526].

Patch, Howard R. *The Goddess Fortuna in Medieval Literature*. New York: Octagon, 1967.

Parker, Henry, Lord Morley. *Forty-Six Lives Translated from Boccaccio's* De Claris Mulieribus. Early English Text Society 214. Oxford: Oxford UP, 1943.

Partner, Nancy F. *Utter Antiquity: Perceptions of Prehistory in Renaissance England*. Durham, NC, and London: Duke UP, 1993.

Patrides, C.A. *The Grand Design of God*. London: Routledge & Kegan Paul, 1972.

Patterson, Annabel. *Reading Holinshed's* Chronicles. Chicago and London: U of Chicago P, 1994.

Peery, William. 'Tragic Retribution in the 1559 *Mirror for Magistrates*.' *Studies in Philology* 46 (1949): 113–30.

Plomer, Henry R. *Wynkyn De Worde & His Contemporaries from the Death of Caxton to 1535*. London: Grafton, 1925.

Primeau, Ronald. 'Daniel and the *Mirror* Tradition: Dramatic Irony in *The Complaint of Rosamond*.' *Studies in English Literature, 1500–1900* 15 (1975): 21–36.

Purkis, G.S. 'Laurent de Premierfait: First French Translator of the *Decameron*.' *Italian Studies* 4 (1949): 22–36.

Rackin, Phyllis. *Stages of History: Shakespeare's English Chronicles*. Ithaca, NY: Cornell UP, 1990.

Ramazani, Jahan. 'Chaucer's Monk: The Poetics of Abbreviation, Aggression, and Tragedy.' *Chaucer Review* 27 (1993): 260–76.

Ribner, Irving. *The English History Play in the Age of Shakespeare*. Rev. ed. New York: Barnes & Noble, 1965.

Robertson, D.W. Jr. 'Chaucerian Tragedy.' Rpt. in *Chaucer Criticism*, vol. 2. Ed. Richard J. Schoeck and Jerome Taylor. Notre Dame, IL: Notre Dame UP, 1961. 86–121.

Rollins, Hyder F. *Old English Ballads, 1553–1625*. Cambridge: Cambridge UP, 1920.

Scanlon, Larry. 'The King's Two Voices: Narrative and Power in Hoccleve's *Regement of Princes*.' In *Literary Practice and Social Change in Britain, 1380–1530*. Ed. Lee Patterson. Berkeley: U of California P, 1990. 216–47.

– *Narrative, Authority, and Power: The Medieval Exemplum and the Chaucerian Tradition*. Cambridge: Cambridge UP, 1994.

Schellhase, Kenneth C. *Tacitus in Renaissance Political Thought*. Chicago and London: U of Chicago P, 1976.

Seymour, M.C. 'Chaucer's Early Poem *De Casibus Virorum Illustrium*.' *Chaucer Review* 24/2 (1989): 163–5.

Shakespeare, William. *The Complete Works*. Ed. David Bevington. 4th ed. New York: HarperCollins, 1992.

– *King Richard II*. Ed. Peter Ure. London: Methuen, 1961.

Sidney, Sir Philip. *The Prose Works*, vol. 3. Ed. Albert Feuillerat. Cambridge: Cambridge UP, 1962.

Socola, Edward M. 'Chaucer's Development of Fortune in the "Monk's Tale."' *Journal of English and Germanic Philology* 49 (1950): 159–71.

Spenser, Edmund. *The Works of Edmund Spenser: A Variorum Edition. The Prose Works*. Ed. Edwin Greenlaw, Charles Gorvesnor Osgood, Frederick Morgan Padelford, and Ray Heffner. Baltimore: Johns Hopkins UP, 1949.

Spufford, Margaret. *Small Books and Pleasant Histories*. London: Methuen, 1981.

Stauffer, Donald A. *English Biography before 1700*. New York: Russell & Russell, 1964.

Strange, William C. 'The *Monk's Tale*: A Generous View.' *Chaucer Review* 1 (1967): 167–80.

Stump, Donald V. 'Sidney's Concept of Tragedy in the *Apology* and in the *Arcadia*.' *Studies in Philology* 79 (1982): 41–61.

Thomas, Keith. *The Perception of the Past in Early Modern England*. London: U of London P, 1983.

Utley, Francis. *The Crooked Rib*. New York: Octagon, 1970.

Ward, A.W., and A.R. Waller, eds. *The Cambridge History of English Literature,* vol. 3. Cambridge: Cambridge UP, 1918.

Warnicke, Retha M. 'Eulogies for Women: Public Testimony of Their Godly Example and Leadership.' In *Attending to Women in Early Modern England.* Ed. Betty S. Travitsky and Adele F. Seeff. Newark: U of Delaware P; London and Toronto: Associated UP, 1994. 168–186.

Watt, Tessa. *Cheap Print and Popular Piety, 1550–1640.* Cambridge: Cambridge UP, 1991.

Whigham, Frank. *Ambition and Privilege: The Social Tropes of Elizabethan Courtesy Theory.* Berkeley: U of California P, 1984.

Williams, Franklin B., Jr. *Index of Dedications and Commendatory Verses in English Books before 1641.* London: Bibliographical Society, 1962.

Woodbridge, Linda. *Women and the English Renaissance.* Urbana and Chicago: U of Illinois P, 1984.

Woolf, Daniel. 'The "Common Voice": History, Folklore and Oral Tradition in Early Modern England.' *Past & Present* no. 120 (Aug. 1988): 26–52.

– 'Of Danes and Giants: Popular Beliefs about the Past in Early Modern Europe.' *Dalhousie Review* 71 (1991): 166–209.

– *The Idea of History in Early Stuart England: Erudition, Ideology, and 'The Light of Truth' from the Accession of James I to the Civil War.* Toronto: U of Toronto P, 1990.

Wright, Herbert G. *Boccaccio in England from Chaucer to Tennyson.* London: Athlone, 1957.

Wright, Louis B. *Middle-Class Culture in Elizabethan England.* Chapel Hill: U of North Carolina P, 1935.

Zocca, Louis R. *Elizabethan Narrative Poetry.* New Brunswick, NJ: Rutgers UP, 1950.

Index